TV VIOLENCE AND THE CHILD

TV VIOLENCE AND THE CHILD

The Evolution and Fate
of the Surgeon General's Report

DOUGLASS CATER *and* **STEPHEN STRICKLAND**

RUSSELL SAGE FOUNDATION   New York

PUBLICATIONS OF RUSSELL SAGE FOUNDATION

Russell Sage Foundation
230 Park Avenue, New York, N.Y. 10017
© 1975 Russell Sage Foundation. All Rights Reserved.
Library of Congress Catalog Card Number: 74-83207
Standard Book Number: 87154-230-X
Printed in the United States of America

To Ben, Pamela, and Jonathan,
and the
coming generations of TV watchers

CONTENTS

ACKNOWLEDGMENTS

We gratefully acknowledge the generous aid and advice of those involved in the Surgeon General's Quest. We appreciate most particularly the diligent research assistance of Maria Savage and the secretarial skills of Susan Sanders and Zene Krogh.

INTRODUCTION

In the early spring of 1969, Senator John Pastore sent a letter to the Secretary of Health, Education and Welfare (HEW) stating that he was "exceedingly troubled by the lack of any definitive information which would help resolve the question of whether there is a causal connection between televised crime and violence and antisocial behavior by individuals, especially children."[1] The Rhode Island senator, a major congressional figure in matters of communications policy, requested that the Surgeon General appoint a committee of distinguished men and women "from whatever professions and disciplines deemed appropriate"[2] to conduct a study which "will establish scientifically insofar as possible what harmful effects, if any, [television] programs have on children."[3] Pastore felt that the Surgeon General should be given this assignment "because of the outstanding contribution made by his Committee through its report on Smoking and Health."[4] He expressed hope of a report within a year's time.

Behind Pastore's request lay years of sporadic debate in and out of Congress about television's contribution to the rising violence in the nation. There was a widespread feeling that the television industry, despite repeated promises, had done very little either to examine television's influence on the young or to reduce the violence content of the programs carried over its networks.

The senator's letter triggered an inquiry lasting nearly three years, ultimately costing over $1.8 million. When the Surgeon General issued his Scientific Advisory Committee's Report, *Television and Growing Up: The Impact of Televised Violence,* in January 1972, it was undergirded by twenty-three independent research projects and more than forty technical papers.

Long before the Report was issued, it was destined for critical review by at least three constituencies. Among social scientists, skepticism had been stirred when Surgeon General William Stewart, claiming the precedent of the Smoking Committee, appointed five employees or consultants of the networks to his new twelve-member Committee on Television and Social Behavior and further allowed the industry to veto the appointment of seven distinguished social scientists who had been doing research in this area. The broadcast industry, on the other hand, was known to be highly suspicious that television was being made the scapegoat for society's ills. And a number of politicians and others were wary lest the findings be inconclusive in an endeavor for which so much time and money was being expended. Five months before the Report was delivered to him, Pastore declared: " . . . I would hope that the Surgeon General in due time will come before this committee, not with a lot of ifs and buts but will tell us in simple language whether or not broadcasters ought to be put on notice and be very, very careful in this area, because it might have an effect on certain people."[5]

The initial results, perhaps predictably, tended to confirm the fears of all three groups. Written in a social-sciencese which made it almost incomprehensible to the layman, the Report displayed a caution which angered a number of critics, including some of the social scientists who had helped carry out the research. Nonetheless, to the discomfort of the industry, the Surgeon General's Committee unanimously found "preliminary" and "tentative" indications of a "causal relation" between viewing televised violence and aggressive behavior. To the dismay of some policymakers, the Committee members were unable to conclude how many children were likely to be affected or what should be done about it.

What ensued was even more disturbing. The Surgeon General's Report was grossly misinterpreted by *The New York Times* and other organs of the media. A battle broke out between critics and defenders. Amid the confused publicity, the credibility of the whole enterprise was threatened until Pastore managed by skillfully conducted Senate hearings to hammer out a consensus: the Report did, indeed, represent significant scientific findings; it should be a cause for public concern; and the television industry should take steps to remove "gratuitous violence" from the programs children watch. Even the network heads appeared to join the chorus of affirmation at the Pastore hearings. HEW agreed to take steps to develop a violence "profile" as a way of measuring performance. Dean Burch, chairman of the Federal Communications Commission (FCC), promised to "hold the TV industry's feet to the fire."

That was the high-water mark. At the time of this writing—two years since those initial hearings—there has been less than persuasive evidence that the commitments given to Pastore have been met with alacrity. Violence on the television screen, according to analysts, has continued at a high level. Violent incidents on prime time and Saturday morning programs maintain a rate of more than twice the British rate which itself is padded by American imports.[6] It is now estimated that HEW's "profile of violence" will be at least two more years in the making. The FCC has not yet dealt with the issue of violence in children's programming.

Thus promise *still* lies ahead. At a second set of hearings in the spring of 1974, network heads assured Pastore that a great deal was being done to reduce "gratuitous violence." Preview announcements of the fall 1974 schedules appeared to indicate a swing away from violence-prone shows toward family situation dramas. There is also considerable activity indicating that the industry is giving higher priority to children's programming. The prospects sound hopeful. Yet, no one can be certain whether this will be an enduring trend or simply one more cyclical swing caused by the faddist nature of the competition among the networks.

Whatever the short-term fallout, there continues to be fundamental disagreement about the meaning of the Surgeon General's Report. Broadcast leaders, while speaking guardedly in the presence of Pastore, disagree with the findings and are busily accumulating contrary evidence. As television reaches its quarter-century anniversary as a major environmental phenomenon in

America, we still know remarkably little about its effects on social behavior. There is even ridicule of the notion that social science has anything to offer such an assessment. According to one leading scholar, writing while the Surgeon General's Report was in preparation,

> In the cases of violence and obscenity, it is unlikely that social science can either show harmful effects or prove that there are no harmful effects. . . . These are moral issues and ultimately all judgments about the acceptability of restrictions on various media will have to rest on political and philosophical considerations.[7]

While the Surgeon General's Committee was still laboring, we became interested in making our own critical assessment. We wished to learn how those responding to Senator Pastore went about their mission and what the consequences would be. They had undertaken a major social science quest—in the tradition of Gunnar Myrdal's inquiry into racial equality and James Coleman's study of educational opportunity—searching for answers to a fundamental societal dilemma. The Aspen Institute's Program on Communications and Society, supported by Russell Sage Foundation, has, through interviews and two conferences, conducted an inquiry into this endeavor.

While the final consequences may not be known for years to come, the following chapters represent the chronicle of the initial stages. Our investigation has been an unsettling experience, for the overwhelming conclusion has been how ill-equipped are this nation's institutions for recruiting expert talent, providing clear findings, and carrying out enlightened objectives in an area of such delicate human concern. As a society, we have become rather accomplished in calling on the technologist for advice to meet material needs. In the case of the Surgeon General's Committee on Smoking, the health professionals gave precise answers which led to concrete acts of public policy.* Yet, in this arena of controversy which rouses elemental fears—both of television's effects on social behavior and of government's threat to freedom of com-

---

*One can raise the caveat that government prohibits cigarette advertising on television but continues to subsidize tobacco growers; and that public addiction to smoking, except among doctors, has not been notably affected.

munications—we are still amateurs when attempting to harness knowledge to public policy and policy to relevant social action.

Without doing damage to the more extended accounting which follows, we should note the troubling uncertainties which dogged the Surgeon General's quest every step of the way. Here follows only a brief listing of the sometimes contradictory dilemmas cited by various observers.

The Senator's Inquiry

Although his letter was phrased with a care not always characteristic of the politician, Senator Pastore raised problems by his sweeping request to the Secretary of Health, Education and Welfare. He suggested a deadline which, though not met, served to speed the investigation through its early stages when more preparation might have avoided subsequent mishaps. It would have helped enormously to negotiate the precise boundaries of the inquiry and to reach prior understanding of the less than absolute answers to be expected from the social scientists.

HEW's Response

Despite its prompt acceptance of Pastore's request, HEW showed grave weaknesses in tackling the assignment. The office of Surgeon General lacked power to give much direction to the task. Political expediencies helped shape the selection of the Scientific Advisory Committee. Bureaucratic caution led to decisions, such as the broadcasters' veto, that damaged the Committee's integrity.

Recruiting Social Science

Prior research into the effects of television provided an insubstantial base on which to build this investigation. Only one study involving children over an extended period of time could be commissioned. Time imposed other severe handicaps. Members of the Surgeon General's Committee, having other commitments, lacked time to develop a cohesive strategy and to perfect the final wording of their conclusions. Prestigious social scientists could not find the time to submit research proposals. It proved difficult for experienced researchers to take the time to serve on the Committee's staff. In brief, what should have been a major public endeavor failed to enlist fully the best skills of social science.

Communicating the Findings

A future social historian exploring this episode will be bewildered by the conflicting interpretations which appeared in the media. Even careful readers of the press found it impossible to learn exactly what the social scientists concluded; television viewers remained almost totally uninformed. One of society's most difficult tasks remains how to communicate complex issues to the public—including issues dealing with our communications system.

Achieving Results

Government operates with questionable effectiveness when pursuing social objectives which, as in the case of television programming, cannot—and should not—be reducible to legislative fiat. The executive agency and the regulatory commission must be wary of activities which could come into conflict with the First Amendment. Congressional hearings provide only sporadic intervention. This means that a large area of social concern falls outside social management.

Citizen Action

The most immediate results in the area of television programming have stemmed from demands of organized groups: parents, blacks and other ethnic groups, and women's rights advocates. Both the television licensee and the advertiser have shown a capacity to listen when aroused citizens speak. But this, too, raises dilemmas of public policy, for the citizens who are likely to speak most forcibly are minorities united around a grievance. Such concentrated pressure group activity may help to curtail abuses, but it may also discourage the freedom and diversity in which creative television can flourish.

To recite the complaints surrounding the Surgeon General's quest tends to convey an entirely bleak picture. We hope that the ensuing chronicle helps to rectify this imbalance. The facts are not all negative: Senator Pastore did manage to trigger a major in-quiry. The social science research was impressive in its totality. Despite many travails, the Surgeon General's Scientific Advisory Committee reached unanimous, if not altogether unambiguous, conclusions. The television industry was put on notice. And the redoubtable senator from Rhode Island has vowed to keep pursu-ing this matter year after year. The public appears to be more conscious that televised violence represents a serious issue.

Only time will reveal whether the cumulative experience of the Surgeon General's quest produces constructive results. There is bound to be a large element of the unpredictable in such an undertaking. Press misinterpretations of the Report, for example, prompted the Surgeon General and members of his Scientific Ad-visory Committee to restate their conclusions more emphatically than they may have first intended. The disputes between critics and defenders resulted in calling greater public attention to the findings. Thus, unplanned happenings have had at least as much impact as those that were planned.

Public policy is usually a confusing business. It would be im-possible for institutions to function with complete tidiness in an endeavor having so many values in conflict. How to encourage television's potential for social good and to discourage its harmful uses will remain a controversial question no matter what social science has to say on the subject; nor do we suggest that social scientists should have the final word. But our study convinces us that the process by which social science is recruited and its findings made relevant to public policy stands in need of improvement.

ORIGINS OF CONCERN

From its beginnings as an object of fascination, television soon became an object of concern. Clearly, it was an instrument of potential power, of pervasive influence. Admiration for technology's achievement in developing this system of communication was accompanied by apprehension about the way it would be used. E. B. White, the essayist, expressed deep concern after watching a television experiment in 1938:

> Television will enormously enlarge the eye's range and, like radio, will advertise the Elsewhere. . . . More hours in every twenty-four will be spent digesting ideas, sounds, images—distant and concocted. . . . A door closing, heard over the air; a face contorted, seen in a panel of light—these will emerge as the real and the true; and when we bang the door of our own cell or look into another's face the impression will be of mere artifice.[1]

America's relationship with the medium of television over the last quarter century has reflected both appreciation and fear. Almost all Americans have succumbed to its lure. In 1948, there were barely 100,000 television sets in use in the United States.[2] By 1973, 96 percent of the homes in the United States had one or more television sets,[3] and the average set was estimated to be turned on for more than six hours a day.[4]

Much of the early concern voiced about the effects of television related to its impact on children. Twenty years ago the National Association of Educational Broadcasters reported that drama involving crime and horror made up 10 percent of programming time.[5] The percentage was considerably higher if "Westerns," with their gunsmoke and barroom fights, were included as drama. The survey underlying that report, funded by the Ford Foundation, was one of only a few research projects relating to television and children.

Parents did not wait for research reports to reach the conclusion that television programs contained much that was unhealthy for their children. Their expressions of disapproval together with objections voiced by educators led to the first congressional hearings on the subject. In 1954, Senator Estes Kefauver, chairman of the Subcommittee on Juvenile Delinquency, conducted an investigation focusing on crime and sex as well as on violence in program content. The Kefauver subcommittee concluded that such programming in large doses could be potentially harmful to young viewers.[6]

Television broadcast industry spokesmen acknowledged the large amount of televised violence and indicated that something would be done about it. But subsequent surveys revealed that the amount of televised violence increased rather than decreased between the early 1950s and the early 1960s.[7] Parents' groups and others stepped up efforts to organize public opinion and secure remedial action against the violence "messages" transmitted by a medium which was an ever-growing presence in the home.

A number of social commentators agreed with the parents. "There can be no real doubt," wrote Walter Lippmann, "that the movies and television and the comic books are purveying violence and lust to a vicious and intolerable degree. . . . Nor can there be any real doubt that there is a close connection between the suddenness in the increase in sadistic crimes and the new vogue of sadism among the mass media of entertainment."[8]

But the judgment of parents and social critics could be only speculative. As of 1960, three of the very small number of experts in the fields of communications, education, and psychology who had examined the specific issue of children's use of television in the United States summed up the state of research:

For it is unfortunately the case that, not only have we been unable to answer the challenging final questions, such as, does television cause delinquency, and does it make for more knowledge or more ignorance; but also we have understood very little the process by which television had an effect, so that we could predict the part it would play in the lives of children.[9]

Reporting on their own research, Wilbur Schramm, Jack Lyle, and Edwin Parker of the Stanford University Department of Communication concluded:

For *some* children, under *some* conditions, *some* television is harmful. For *other* children under the same conditions, or for the same children under *other* conditions, it may be beneficial. For *most* children, under *most* conditions, *most* television is probably neither particularly harmful nor particularly beneficial.[10]

The Senate Subcommittee on Juvenile Delinquency conducted surveys of television program content in 1961 and again in 1964 and reported "that the extent to which violence and related activities are depicted on television . . . remains greater than it was a decade ago." Senator Thomas Dodd commented: "Not only did we fail to see an appreciable reduction of violence in new shows, but we also found that the most violent shows of the 1961–62 season have been syndicated and are now being reshown on independent networks and stations."[11]

The 1964 Senate Subcommittee report warned that such television content produced antisocial behavior among juveniles and repeated the charge of psychiatrist Frederic S. Wertham, in his book *Seduction of the Innocent,* that "television was becoming a school for violence."[12]

For its part, the television industry seemed unimpressed by these congressional findings, nor were demands of angry parents sufficient indicators of consumer attitudes to prompt changes. On the contrary, the activity of the marketplace suggested that television's program content was satisfying both viewers and sponsors. Growing millions of Americans were watching, including children who watched adult programs with tacit approval of parents.

That phenomenon was of particular concern to one social scientist exploring the effects of the mass media. Joseph Klapper, then with the General Electric Company and later to become CBS director of research, warned in 1959 of possible adverse consequences from allowing children to spend much of their time watching adult programs:

Adult fare deals almost exclusively with adults, and usually with adults in conflict situations. Some psychologists and psychiatrists feel that continued exposure to such fare might unnaturally accelerate the impact of the adult environment on the child and force him into a kind of premature maturity, marked by bewilderment, distrust of adults, a superficial approach to adult problems, and even unwillingness to become an adult.[13]

By the middle 1960s, television had become for many children an environment in itself, so total was its programming and so available. If there were potential dangers to children, no one was certain which kinds of programs or what quantities were dangerous. At least, there was not sufficient proof to convince either those who produced programs or most of those who watched.

The assassinations and riots of the middle 1960s prompted a serious effort to search out the causes of violence in our society. President Lyndon Johnson, appointing the National Commission on the Causes and Prevention of Violence, charged it to undertake a "penetrating search . . . into our national life, our past as well as our present, our traditions as well as our institutions, our culture, our customs and our laws"[14] in order to explain and propose remedies for any persistent forces at work in American society which were productive of violence. The Commission, chaired by Dr. Milton Eisenhower, set up a Task Force on the Media.

The Eisenhower Commission, originally given a year starting in June 1968 to complete its work, had its life extended by President Richard Nixon until December 1969. Because of these limits of time the Commission did not attempt to undertake major new research other than to order a survey of TV program content. In developing its report, it instead relied principally on the opinions and recommendations of "the best minds in the communications media, especially in television; in the academic community, particularly communications specialists; and in government agencies, notably the Federal Communications Commission."[15] There was an effort, under research director James Short, a sociologist, to bring together major findings of researchers of various disciplines in fields potentially relevant to this investigation. Actually, very few research projects had focused specifically on television and its effects, though a number of studies considered pertinent had involved the use of films as research tools. The Commission, while warning of the danger of making television a "scapegoat," issued a strong statement on televised violence:

We believe it is reasonable to conclude that a constant diet of violent behavior on television has an adverse effect on human character and attitudes. Violence on television encourages violent forms of behavior, and fosters moral and social values about violence in daily life which are unacceptable in a civilized society . . . it is a matter for grave concern that at a time when the values and the influence of traditional institutions such as family, church, and school are in question, television is emphasizing violent, antisocial styles of life.[16]

A Commission staff report on "Mass Media and Violence" was more pointed in assigning responsibility for remedying the situation. Stating that "there is sufficient evidence that mass media presentations, especially portrayals of violence, have negative effects upon audiences," the staff recommended "that the burden of research and proof be placed squarely on the mass media, especially commercial television, to carry out meaningful research on the psychological and social effects of mass media portrayals of violence."[17] For the previous fifteen years, stated the report, the television industry had failed to reduce the violence content of programs despite repeated promises to do so. Moreover, despite repeated promises, the television industry had conducted no significant research. " . . . Although such promises were made first in 1954 and continued through 1964, by October 1967 the amount of research sponsored by the industry on this issue was so small as to be insignificant and that which was supported by the industry was, from the outset, clearly undertaken as a defensive move."[18]

The Media Task Force staff added one other note:

The public has tremendous powers to bring about changes in mass media content that are held by no governmental agency. The source of the public's power derives directly from the fact that modern mass media organizations are economic in nature and orientation, and are directly dependent upon the public for their economic welfare.[19]

It was a warning to the industry of the power of citizen action already in the making. In 1968, even as the Eisenhower Commission was beginning its work, three women in Newtonville, Massachusetts, decided that something had to be done to stop the commercial exploitation of children on television shows designed especially for them. They particularly objected to the stars or hosts of children's shows urging the young viewers to buy the products of the programs' sponsors. Calling themselves Action for Children's Television (ACT), the three women—Evelyn Sarson, Peggy

Charren, and Judith Chalfen—urged the producers of "Romper Room" to discontinue the practice by which the "teacher-hostess" of that show also pushed the "Romper Room" line of toys. The producers displayed little sympathy for the proposal.

The practice against which ACT protested was not simply an incidental or thoughtless one. Advertising agencies had been quite candid about how much their clients could benefit by pitching their television commercials straight at the children. One wrote in *Advertising Age* in 1965:

> When you sell a woman on a product and she goes into the store and finds your brand isn't in stock, she'll probably forget about it. But when you sell a kid on your product, if he can't get it, he will throw himself on the floor, stamp his feet and cry. You can't get a reaction like that out of an adult.[20]

Another advertising executive urged in *Broadcasting* in 1969:

> Sooner or later you must look through kids' goggles, see things as they see them, appeal to them through their childish emotions and meet them on their own ground.[21]

In late 1969, ACT petitioned the FCC to issue three new rules for children's television: no commercials on programs for children; no mentioning of products by brand names; and the provision of fourteen hours of commercial-free children's programs each week as a part of each television station's public service requirement. The FCC agreed to consider the petition. Notice of the petition and the Commission's reaction brought an outpouring of public support for ACT. A *Saturday Review* columnist praised the group for having "harnessed a sense of outrage at the commercialization of children's programs."[22] The *Christian Science Monitor* suggested that Action for Children's Television had begun a new movement "which could lead to a crusade as decisive as the public action on auto safety and cigarette advertising."[23] Within a matter of a few months, thousands of citizens had filed comments with the FCC in support of ACT's petition. (By July 1971, the Commission had received 60,000 such comments; by late 1973—with final action still not taken—the number had passed 100,000.) The concern of the citizenry about the impact of television on children reached a new intensity. By the time the Eisenhower Commission's Media Task Force staff pointed out the leverage for change in television programming, the three women from Newtonville had already discovered it.

Before the FCC could act on the formal petition, the producers of some children's shows "voluntarily" ended the practice of having the actors sell the sponsors' products. Having begun to make headway on the problem of commercials, members of ACT turned their efforts to other practices they believed were wrong in the television industry's treatment of children. They focused on violence and inanity in cartoons, and on the dearth of quality programs for children.

Television had also been causing increasing concern to the congressional successors to Estes Kefauver, among them the chairman of the Senate Subcommittee on Communications, John Pastore. This concern of the Rhode Island senator about the quality and effects of television was by no means new. A member of the Subcommittee since entering the Senate in 1951, Pastore became its chairman in 1955. The television quiz scandals in 1958–59 had prompted one of his first hard looks at industry practices, and his hearings sought to produce a remedy for that problem. The remedy was one which would become standard for the senator: he would engage network officials in public discussions, hence subjecting them to informal pressure which would result in self-regulation.

A devoted family man and devout Catholic, Pastore was from an early date worried about sex and violence on television. In an address before the National Association of Broadcasters (NAB) in 1962, he applauded the critics, declaring:

> I want to make it clear that I am not condemning all television programming nor subscribing to the thesis that all crime and violence, blood and thunder programs are the sole and direct cause of juvenile delinquency. But I must agree that this type of program is not conducive to good behavior and does not excite and draw out the best attributes of character in our children and, indeed, even in adults.[24]

Yet Pastore's concern about effects of television programming was always double-edged; he was chary of formal governmental action which might trespass on First Amendment freedoms. In the same speech, Pastore said:

> Congress will not and cannot stand idly by and allow excesses or abuses to dominate this great medium, nor will it be stampeded by the cries of censorship every time an observation of a constructive nature is made to improve the quality of programming. There is no one more than I, myself, who would resist interference with freedom of expression.

On the other hand, it is well to remember that there is one distinguishing factor that separates the broadcasting system from almost every business in the United States—that is, a condition that the broadcaster must operate in the public interest.[25]

What he was proposing was self-examination and self-control: "I would urge the entire broadcasting industry to take a new, long, hard look at itself and at its practices, particularly in programming."[26]

The assassinations and riots later in the decade affected Senator Pastore as they did President Johnson and other Americans. Becoming increasingly disturbed, Pastore intensified his attention to television violence as something which, given his position, he might perhaps be able to influence. There were, he knew, other policymaking bodies working on the subject, including the Eisenhower Commission's Media Task Force. There also was a Joint Committee for Research on Television and Children, with representatives of HEW and the three major television networks, which had been established at the behest of the Senate Judiciary Committee in 1963. Pastore hoped one or more of these groups would produce clues, if not answers, to the vexing question of whether and to what extent television helped nurture the seeds of violence in American society. The Joint Committee had awarded a planning grant in December 1963 to promote the development of a research design for assessing the general influence of television on children. But as Senator Pastore noted in 1969: "Unfortunately, for whatever reasons, no reports or recommendations have been forthcoming."[27]

Not wishing to intrude on these other efforts, Pastore waited throughout 1968 before taking official steps to act on his concern. However, wanting to be prepared if more had to be done, Pastore directed his staff to begin an informal exploration of the subject. Early in 1968, subcommittee counsel Nicholas Zapple directed his associate, John Hardy, to visit a small number of social scientists around the country. The result was a collection of mixed opinions, but all of them were agreed that the issue was serious. As Zapple recalls, "After our preliminary exploration of the subject, the senator decided that what was needed was a good, solid scientific study. And he wanted a study that would be completed."

By March 1968, it was clear that the Eisenhower Commission

would not issue its report in June. Indeed, there was a rumor that the Commission would not formally address the issue of televised violence, but, instead, release as a staff document the report of the Mass Media Task Force. Thus, on March 5, Senator Pastore was finally provoked to write HEW Secretary Robert Finch, requesting that he direct the Surgeon General to appoint a committee to "devise techniques and to conduct a study . . . which will establish scientifically insofar as possible what harmful effects, if any, these programs have on children." Pastore suggested that the committee be made up of "distinguished men and women from whatever professions and disciplines the Surgeon General deemed appropriate." He asked that the study be completed in a year's time.[28]

Senator Pastore's request gave the secretary great discretion in the way such an advisory committee would be set up. Yet it was clear that he expected social scientists to play a major part in the effort. Citing studies by psychologists, psychiatrists, and those from "other disciplines related to social behavior," Pastore remarked on the "different and divergent views on this subject. . . ." He was, he wrote, "exceedingly troubled by the lack of any definitive information which would help resolve the question of whether there is a causal connection between televised crime and violence and antisocial behavior by individuals, especially children." Social science was to be called on to help resolve a social dilemma of crucial importance. "What is at stake," he wrote, "is no less than our most valuable and trusted resource—the minds and hearts of our young people."[29]

3

THE SURGEON GENERAL'S
ADVISORY COMMITTEE

Government does not always move at a snail's pace. One week after Senator Pastore dispatched his letter to Secretary Finch, the secretary sent the Surgeon General of the Public Health Service, Dr. William H. Stewart, to talk with Pastore and his committee colleagues about the issues that had been raised. Appearing in open hearings of the Senate Subcommittee on Communications, Dr. Stewart agreed with the chairman about "the need to know" and said that the request for a special advisory committee would be acted upon. In fact, Dr. Stewart had already gotten informal advice on the appointment of an advisory panel from colleagues within HEW.[1]

Later the same month, on March 24, 1969, President Nixon wrote to Senator Pastore to express his personal endorsement of the study.

> Dear Senator:
> I want you to know that I join you in supporting the proposed one-year study of the possible relationship between scenes of sex and violence on television and antisocial behavior among young people.
> Your forthright stand is one that reflects the views of very many Americans who are deeply concerned with the ethical as well as the artistic level of many television programs and commercials.

19

The medium of television reaches the widest possible audience in the most intensely personal manner of any of the mass media. I share your deep concern and strongly applaud your vigorous criticism of what you regard as a misuse of this great medium.

As chairman of the Communications Subcommittee of the Senate Commerce Committee, you have indeed served the public interest well by bringing greater public attention to this problem.

Sincerely,
/s/ Richard Nixon

On April 16, Secretary Finch formally authorized the establishment of the Surgeon General's Advisory Committee on Television and Social Behavior; on June 3, the appointment of the body was announced. Rarely had any similar governmental advisory committee been set up so quickly. Not within anyone's memory had a congressional request been agreed to with such enthusiasm. In the rumor mills of the television industry, there was anxious speculation that the Nixon Administration saw an opportunity to gain an advantage in its warfare with the networks.

Much maneuvering had taken place backstage during the preparation period. Delicate procedural questions had to be resolved. In the first place, the government's health hierarchy had been restructured since the early 1960s when the Surgeon General carried out the smoking study. By 1969, the Surgeon General had been superseded by the Assistant Secretary for Health and Scientific Affairs, a political appointee, as the government's chief health officer. The Surgeon General no longer had direct line responsibility for the operations of all of HEW's health-related bureaus, and plans were in motion to reduce his role still further. In this circumstance, an early question was whether giving the new assignment to the Surgeon General might not conflict with these plans.

Another important question was how to finance such a comprehensive research effort. Among all the health-oriented bureaus of the government, none has a more dedicated constituency than the National Institute of Mental Health (NIMH). And no constituency has a more effective lobby organization. Established in 1946 as one of the early components of the National Institutes of Health, NIMH during the next two decades became so strong and independent that by 1967 it was spun off from NIH with the blessing of its "parent." It took with it an annual budget of about a quarter of a billion dollars.[2]

NIMH continued to be more independent of policy and budget (and political) controls than the ordinary federal bureau. With its constituency comprising not only important and well organized academic disciplines, including psychiatry and psychology, but thousands of state and local officials and many thousands more lay citizens, NIMH rarely experienced any reductions in its budget proposals. Quite often, the constituency's chief lobbying organization, the National Committee Against Mental Illness, was able to persuade Congress to add more money than was requested in the president's budget.

NIMH was also wide ranging in its research programs. "Mental health" was such a comprehensive term that the agency could claim a mandate to support studies on subjects as far flung as nutrition and brain cell growth, psychological effects of economic disadvantage, cultural and political implications of prolonged breast-feeding on infants in primitive cultures, and patterns of oral and tactile communications among primates.[3]

This budgetary and programmatic independence of NIMH had been displeasing to those whose positions further up the government's organization chart should have given them supervisory control over the Institute. But in the present case, since NIMH *ought* to be sponsoring research in this area, and since it always had a budget large enough to accommodate an unexpected cost, the HEW hierarchy decided that the bureau should get the assignment.

Thus, the plan worked out in Secretary Finch's office was to appoint Surgeon General Stewart as chairman of the new Advisory Committee, while the vice-chairman and senior staff coordinator would be Dr. Eli Rubinstein, a psychologist, who was Assistant Director for NIMH's Extra-Mural Programs.[4] (The Secretary showed his personal interest in the Committee by appointing as liaison his special consultant, Richard A. Moore, former president and general manager of a Los Angeles television station.) NIMH was to serve as the "central resource" for the Advisory Committee, and ultimately provide approximately $1 million for new research and another $500,000 for administrative expenses. That money was squeezed out of existing budgets by the simple device of eliminating or postponing construction projects in the Community Mental Health Center Program. Officials of NIMH appeared pleased to add television and social behavior to their research jurisdiction. Senator Pastore, though somewhat surprised that free money should be found so easily by the bureaucrats, was happy that the inquiry could get underway promptly.

Next came the problem of appointments. Among the various standard procedures for developing candidate lists for government advisory committees, there was the recent precedent of the Surgeon General's Advisory Committee on Smoking and Health whereby the tobacco industry had been allowed to review and comment on those whose names were proposed for membership. The rationale had been that if the Committee subsequently issued an adverse report on cigarette smoking, as in fact it did, no one could complain that it had been prejudiced against the industry. The question was whether the television industry, which might be the target of criticism in the new Advisory Committee's report, should be given a similar opportunity to review candidate lists. On the advice of Dr. Rubinstein, Surgeon General Stewart answered "yes."

A number of organizations representing a spectrum of relevant social science expertise were asked to submit nominations. They included the American Psychological Association, the American Sociological Association, and the American Psychiatric Association. Also asked for nominations were the National Association of Broadcasters (NAB), and the three television networks. The Committee was to be "a little like Noah's Ark," one observer later remarked. "They wanted representatives from every species."[5]

A list of 200 names was compiled from those and other sources. After many reviews and eliminations, a final list of forty names was sent for review to the chief executives of ABC, NBC, CBS, and the NAB. Frank Stanton, president of CBS, responded to the Surgeon General that he thought the nominees were "distinguished," but declined to make suggestions about whom the Surgeon General ought, or ought not, to appoint to his Advisory Committee. Joseph Klapper, CBS director of research, to whom the Surgeon General's letter was first referred, said afterward, "I was astounded when I read that letter."[6] Evidently others felt no such reservations. NBC, ABC, and the NAB did comment on the list, raising objections to seven of the preliminary nominees. Surgeon General Stewart deferred to this industry "veto." In addition, the television industry was allowed other prerogatives. Five of the thirty-five persons nominated by the networks and the NAB were selected to serve on the Advisory Committee. Two of them, Joseph Klapper and Thomas Coffin, were network officials as well as social scientists. The other three had been employed as network consultants.

In the final selection, only one of the twenty-nine persons suggested by the professional and academic organizations was named to the Committee. Matilda B. Paisley, a social scientist at Stanford University, commented in reviewing the selection process: "The final decisions were apparently made with regard for race, sex, political acceptability, and heterogeneity of background."[7] In fact, except for the industry veto, the Committee's selection process was fairly typical of the way government goes about choosing its advisors.

The twelve chosen were:

Ira H. Cisin, Ph.D., Professor of Sociology, George Washington University

Thomas E. Coffin, Ph.D., Vice-President, National Broadcasting Company

Irving L. Janis, Ph.D., Professor of Psychology, Yale University

Joseph T. Klapper, Ph.D., Director of Social Research, Columbia Broadcasting System, Inc.

Harold Mendelsohn, Ph.D., Professor of Mass Communication, and Director, Communication Arts Center, University of Denver

Eveline Omwake, M.A., Professor and Chairman, Department of Child Development, Connecticut College

Charles A. Pinderhughes, M.D., Associate Clinical Professor of Psychiatry, Tufts University, and Lecturer in Psychiatry, Harvard Medical School

Ithiel de Sola Pool, Ph.D., Professor and Chairman, Political Science Department, Massachusetts Institute of Technology

Alberta E. Siegel, Ph.D., Associate Professor of Psychology, Stanford University Medical School

Anthony F. C. Wallace, Ph.D., Professor and Chairman, Department of Anthropology, University of Pennsylvania

Andrew S. Watson, M.D., Professor of Psychiatry and Professor of Law, University of Michigan

Gerhart D. Wiebe, Ph.D., Dean, School of Communications, Boston University

Ten days after their appointments were announced, the members of the Advisory Committee met for the first time. The first ground rule established was one which Secretary Finch had already imposed in his April statement: the Committee will confine its study solely to scientific findings and will make no policy recommendations.[8] Another decision of the Committee reflected an earlier statement of the Surgeon General: it would be inappropriate to take a narrow view of the problem of television and social behavior.[9] Dr. Stewart had said that if television can have negative effects on children, it can also be a positive stimulus. "We must learn more about how to promote this latter capability while we learn to avoid the hazards of the former."[10] The Committee asked that a bibliography of existing research be compiled, and that a continuing index be kept of such research. Further, the Committee recommended that the research be undertaken in two phases: a short-range effort "of a year or two" to try to obtain sound answers to the questions specified; and an on-going research enterprise to develop progressively refined knowledge of the process of child development as it is influenced by exposure to television.[11]

While not adopting a specific operating procedure, the Committee also moved toward another position that would have important consequences. The Committee would not direct the research nor, for that matter, even develop a strategy for approaching the research challenge. Its role was to be that of assessor of results, and it would not, in Dr. Rubinstein's words, "be in charge of operations." The posture of detachment was not taken uniformly; Committee members did discuss the establishment of "liaison groups," to include Committee members and researchers, but this liaison never actually went into operation. It was left to the Committee's staff to define research needs and then to solicit proposals from social scientists designed to meet these needs. This turned out to be a difficult task.

Finding a competent staff to handle these responsibilities

proved to have its own difficulties. Dr. Rubinstein, as chief operating officer of the Committee, felt that only an able social scientist could effectively direct the research effort. Unlike lawyers, who can be fairly rapidly recruited for government work, academicians, whose schedules are ordinarily set at least a year in advance, find it hard to respond to a sudden summons or to make commitments of indeterminate length. The incentives for attracting top scholars to government staff positions are not considerable. While salary levels can sometimes be tempting, staff responsibilities rarely provide an opportunity to pursue established scholarly interests. There is virtually no individual opportunity to "publish"—always a key to academic advancement. Dr. Orville G. Brim, Jr., former president of Russell Sage Foundation, has observed that social scientists get rewards for being "critical," not for being "constructive." Nor do academicians attach the same prestige to government staff posts as they do to membership on governmental commissions or committees. A University of California scholar remarked: "Appointments to important government advisory committees are considered plums; the staff posts are pits."

Dr. Rubinstein was turned down thirty-eight times before he found a senior research coordinator. He finally engaged for that key job a comparatively junior academician, Dr. Douglas A. Fuchs, then serving as assistant professor of journalism at the University of California, Berkeley. Dr. John Robinson of the Survey Research Center of the University of Michigan was chosen as a second "coordinator." Meanwhile, Dr. Rubinstein, attempting to locate social scientists who might perform the actual research, found that a number of the senior ones had work already underway so they felt obliged to decline the invitation to submit proposals. The Surgeon General later reported to the Pastore Committee that, during the summer of 1969, "invitations were extended to fifty research organizations and to about one hundred key research scientists to participate in the program."[12]

Staff differences developed at the outset. Dr. Fuchs felt strongly that the only way to get the job done was to mount a carefully designed, centrally coordinated research effort. The most important research questions and research gaps should be identified; then specific proposals should be invited which would provide directly responsive information. Each of the studies funded, he believed, must be related to each of the others; and the methodologies must be compatible if not identical.[13]

A different approach, favored by Dr. Rubinstein, would be to issue open-ended research invitations to the scientific community, and to accept and fund those proposals which looked interesting and original and relevant. There were several arguments for taking this tack. In the first place, the tradition of NIMH (as well as the National Institutes of Health) has been to let the investigator define the scientific problem, or at least define the way in which his proposed research would relate to a generic problem. Second, there was a fear that narrowing or structuring the questions too rigidly would be tantamount to "putting all the eggs in one basket." If the basket turned out to have flaws—if the research design had conceptual weaknesses—the whole effort could be seriously damaged.

There was still another reason for taking a less structured approach to the studies to be done. In the word of one social scientist, the reason was "politics:"

> Not in any venal sense, you understand. It's just that when a fair amount of money becomes available to support research in a given field, there is an awful lot of politicking among the academicians for cutting up the pie. Everybody wants some, and he wants it to do things *he* thinks are important.[14]

The geographic imperative also comes into play in spending research money. If the single most important research question is identified in advance as being patterns of television use by small children, and most of the best researchers who have worked on that problem are at a single institution, ideally most of the research money should go to those researchers at that institution. But when a million dollars from the public purse are involved, few bureaucrats are willing to risk the political heat by concentrating the bulk of those funds in a single educational institution or even in a single geographical area.

During periods when federal research budgets are growing, this kind of conflict is less difficult to resolve. The decade 1958 to 1968—beginning with the United States' response to *Sputnik* and ending when Vietnam war costs began to block increases in the federal government's domestic budget—was one of steady growth for biomedical and social science funds. In that decade, the National Institutes of Health and the National Science Foundation took special care to "invest" in the developing research competence of less prestigious institutions. (Occasional prodding from President Johnson helped the trend along.) By 1969, when the Surgeon General's study was getting underway, the "geographic imperative" was fully operative even as federal research budgets had begun to level off.*

A final reason advanced for the less structured approach to research was that an open-ended invitation would probably identify and encourage younger scholars in the field, whereas a closed bid would almost certainly result in contracts for only the more prominent few.

The issue—a strongly controlled, sharply focused research plan versus a looser strategy—was discussed by the staff throughout the summer of 1969. (One approach, dismissed out of hand, was the proposal by a consulting firm to take over the whole job for $1 million, and, by staging a series of conferences, provide a "scientific answer" to Senator Pastore's questions.) What the Advisory Committee approved in September was the looser strategy. In fact, it turned out to be so loose that it could hardly be called a strategy.

Although they eschewed a role in setting priorities, the Committee felt no compunction about severely criticizing the approach advanced by coordinator Fuchs. Indeed, the criticisms at the September meeting were so caustic, Fuchs and several associates talked of resigning. Eli Rubinstein, a consummate diplomat,

---

*In 1960, Senator Hubert Humphrey raised the issue of geographic distribution of federal research and development funds with the Assistant Secretary of Defense for Research and Engineering.

> Senator Humphrey: . . . I notice that a tremendous amount of research finds its way into certain selected areas. Now the answer to that, when I write a letter [to get an explanation] is, "Well, these are the people who have the competence. These are the institutions, the universities, the businesses that have the competence in this area." How did they get the competence? They got it when you gave them the first contract.
> Mr. Rubel: My only comment, Mr. Chairman, is that first you used the words selected areas. . . . And I would like to emphasize again that there is no such thing as selected areas. We don't select by area (Select Committee on Small Business, Hearings before the Subcommittee on Governmental Procurement, U.S. Senate, 86th Congress, 2nd Session, April 7, 1960, pp. 28–29).

Today, no federal science official would make such a flat statement.

managed to calm the anger, at least temporarily, and developed a description of the emerging research strategy that offered hope of a purposeful, coordinated outcome:

> The framing of the total research program is complicated. Staff members are making a special effort to develop as much interrelationship and integration of the individual studies as possible. Where appropriate, common measuring instruments will be used. . . . It is also anticipated that the various investigators collaborating with the total research program will be called in from time to time to discuss mutual problems.[15]

Some of the researchers whose projects were approved did meet together in Washington following the Advisory Committee's second meeting in September 1969. The specific purpose was to get acquainted with each other's research plans with the hope that such acquaintance would induce greater "interrelationship." At least one of the social scientists present, Jack Lyle, feared it might not work. Listening to his colleagues describe what they intended to do and how they intended to do it, he suddenly felt "very depressed."

> I said to a member of the staff: "There has been a very major mistake. What you should have done is to have one big study. What you're going to end up with now is so goddamn many little pieces that you can't put them together."[16]

4

WHAT THE RESEARCHERS FOUND:
IN THE LAB

A truly complete understanding of the exact effects of violence portrayed in the mass media is a goal for researchers to aim for, but, realistically, it is a goal that will probably never be reached.[1]

With that caveat, the report of the Task Force on Mass Media and Violence of the Eisenhower Commission in 1969 offered a summary of what research had shown about the effects on children of media violence:

1. Learning Effects

Novel, aggressive behavior sequences are learned by children through exposure to realistic portrayals of aggression on television or in films. A large proportion of these behaviors are retained over long periods of time if they are practiced at least once. The likelihood that such aggressive behaviors will be performed is determined, in part, by the similarity of the setting of the observed violence and the cues present in later situations. The actual performance of aggressive behaviors learned from the media is largely contingent on the child's belief in the effectiveness of aggression in attaining his goals while avoiding punishment. The mass media typically present aggression as a highly effective form of behavior.

2. Emotional Effects

Frequent exposure produces an emotional habituation to media violence. There is suggestive evidence that this results in an increased likelihood of actually engaging in aggression.

3. Impulsive Aggression

Aggressive impulses may be held in check if the viewer has been made especially aware of the 'wrongness' of aggression or of the suffering that may result from violence. The target person's prior association with media violence serves to heighten the intensity of aggressive attacks on him.[2]

The research review leading to this summary cited approximately two dozen empirical studies, representing the work of no more than a dozen individual researchers or research teams. Professor Albert Bandura and his colleagues at Stanford University and Professor Leonard Berkowitz and his colleagues at the University of Wisconsin together had conducted more than half of the experiments relied upon. All the cited studies had involved films as research tools, but none apparently had employed actual television sequences or programs. The only research mentioned which had specific reference to the effects of television were a 1958 survey study of media effects by British scholar Hilda Himmelweit and her colleagues, and a book, *Violence in the Mass Media*, edited by Professor Otto Larsen.

These few studies—along with other studies of learning behavior, emotional reaction, motivation, etc., which were not focused on the mass media—caused the Task Force to reach certain judgments. Acknowledging that the evidence was incomplete, it concluded: "The weight of social science research stands in opposition to the conclusion that mass media portrayals of violence have no effect upon individuals, groups and society."[3] Moreover, it stated: "Of all the mass media, television portrayals of violence have the greatest potential for short and long term effects upon audiences."[4]

The research relied upon by the Commission was not as persuasive to others, including some social scientists. Apart from the question of whether the effects of television could be projected when no actual television programs had been used in the research, there was the more general question of the applicability of laboratory research to the real world. Almost all the research findings cited were produced in "laboratories."

The Eisenhower Commission Task Force had itself pointed out the problem with the laboratory experiments: "Typically, the subjects studied in a given experiment have been drawn from a relatively narrow group [rather than] a completely representative sample of subjects drawn from all areas of the general population."[5] A second problem related to the settings and conditions of the experiments. As the Task Force acknowledged, some of the most important laboratory research had been done throughout the decade of the 1960s by Professor Bandura and his colleagues. One of Bandura's studies, reported in 1963, is typical in its setting, sample of children, and situation.[6]

Children in a nursery school individually watched an adult attack a large, rounded, inflated plastic doll about four feet tall, painted to look like Bobo the Clown. The doll was weighted so that it returned to an upright position when struck. Divided into three groups, the children witnessed the adult—either live, on film, or in a "television sequence"—punch the doll in the face, kick it, or strike it with a hammer. A fourth group of children, serving as a control group, saw none of the aggressive actions.

Shortly after witnessing one of the sequences, all of the children were subjected to a frustrating situation. They were given toys to play with; the toys were then suddenly and arbitrarily taken away. Next, the children were taken to a room where they could play with, among other things, the Bobo doll. During the ensuing twenty minutes, the children's actions were monitored, and a record kept of each one's acts of "imitative" behavior (kicking, punching, or striking the Bobo doll with a hammer), "partially imitative" behavior, and "non-imitative" aggressive actions. The children who had witnessed the aggressive actions by the adult were much more aggressive—frequently imitating the adult's exact techniques of aggression—than were those who had not viewed the original "aggression."

But, skeptics might ask, when would a child find himself in such a situation: be allowed to observe a novel action on film, be pointedly frustrated or provoked, and finally be provided the chance to take out his frustration in the same manner and on the same object that he had just observed? Because a child would strike a plastic doll, does that mean he would be as likely to strike another human being?

Professor Bandura responded that prize fighters learn and hone their pugilistic skills on punching bags and sparring partners, not on other boxers whom they intend to hurt. Before we send troops into war zones, we train them to plunge bayonets into stuffed canvas dummies, not into other soldiers. Bandura argued: "If aggressive repertoires were taught only while individuals were hostilely aroused and entertained injurious designs, many of the tutors and the learners would probably be maimed in the process."

There are other arguments to be made on both sides of the question of the utility of laboratory research. The point here is that when the Surgeon General's Advisory Committee began its task, most of the research evidence suggesting adverse effects of filmed violence on children had been developed in laboratory-like situations under "unnatural" conditions. For that reason, the evidence was not considered conclusive.

Indeed, in 1969, virtually the only research findings not in serious dispute were (1) that there was violence, and (2) that violent programs pervaded the televised airways. Counting only explicit threats or acts of violence, George Gerbner developed data for the Eisenhower Commission which showed that 81.3 percent of the entertainment programs offered by the three major networks during prime time viewing hours in 1967 contained violence. In 1968, the year which brought the assassinations of Dr. Martin Luther King and Senator Robert F. Kennedy, the volume of violent programming rose to 81.6 percent.[7] The Mass Media Task Force stated: "If television is compared to a meal, programming containing violence clearly is the main course being served."[8]

Assuming that televised cartoons have relatively exclusive children's audiences, Gerbner found that 94.3 percent of programs with a cartoon format contained violence in 1967, with an average of 21.6 violent episodes per hour. The number of cartoon programs including aggressive actions dropped slightly in 1968, but the number of violent episodes in all cartoon programs increased to 23.5 per hour.[9]

These statistics were offered in the context of three other sets of undisputed figures. For most children, television occupies as many or more hours than school during their first sixteen years. Secondly, in the national survey Louis Harris conducted for the Eisenhower Commission, 59 percent of the sample of adult citizens surveyed thought there was too much violence in entertainment programs. Sixty-three percent disapproved of the kind of volence portrayed.[10] In short, there was no question about the amount of exposure to televised violence that most American children experienced. But "Exposure alone does not automatically mean that the viewer will be affected";[11] nor in what ways, nor to what degree, nor for how long.

What was required, as the Surgeon General's Committee began its task in the summer of 1969, was "a comprehensive research effort." Dr. Stewart reported to Senator Pastore that the Committee "is exploring many phases of the process of transmitting and receiving televised communications: in the clinical laboratory and natural settings, on both the child and his milieu, both physical and verbal violence, televised violence in both real and fantasy form, and recognizing positive and negative elements in this powerful form of mass communication."[12]

The twenty-three research projects supported by the Television and Social Behavior Program—as the NIMH designated its effort for the Surgeon General's Committee—encompassed a variety of research techniques and focuses. Many of the projects were built on earlier efforts. Typically, the researchers attempted to refine techniques and measurements as well as to clarify or extend previous results. Apart from further work on content analysis and viewing patterns, and new surveys of attitudes of program producers, writers, and network officials, the research on the effects of television could be divided into two broad approaches or methods: in the laboratory and in the field.

The field approach, which the Committee described as "applying the concepts and data gathering techniques of field social survey research," assumed special importance.[13] While laboratory research could not be slighted, the Committee recognized that "the study of television's effects on social behavior is not easily approached solely by examination in a laboratory setting."[14]

Elaborating on the shortcomings of laboratory studies identified by the Eisenhower Commission, the Committee said:

> To varying degrees, depending on design and procedures, they have the disadvantages of artificiality and constricted time span. The generalizability of results to everyday life is a question often not easily resolvable.[15]

Yet the Committee also argued: "Experiments have the advantage of allowing causal inference because various influences can be controlled so that the effects, if any, of one or more variables can be assessed."[16]

In the end, the aggregate results of all the research comprised the most impressive evidence for the Committee. But the settings, processes, and results of some of the individual projects are fascinating in themselves. Moreover, it is important for those concerned with the question of television violence and children to know what the professional researchers did, and how they did it, since their work produced the raw material for the Committee's judgments.

What follows is a selective description of some of the projects which composed the Television and Social Behavior Program. Essentially the projects summarized are important either because they represented new research approaches, or produced new results, or advanced understanding of long-standing questions or issues, including some very controversial ones.

Professor Robert Liebert, a psychologist at the Fels Institute, had as his major scientific interest the matter of observational learning—how and what children learn from others and when and under what circumstances they put into use what they have learned. He was impressed with the Bandura studies, but he thought an important question was still unanswered. "You couldn't be sure from those studies whether the fact that a child would imitate hitting a plastic clown meant he would also hit a person, or not."[17] With several colleagues, he ran a series of studies that proved to his satisfaction "that children would imitate aggression against another person."[18]

The research results of Dr. Liebert and his colleagues were reported "in the literature"—for example, in the publications of the American Psychological Association in 1969. The Advisory Committee staff, aware of the reports, asked Liebert whether he was interested in submitting a proposal. With a colleague, Dr. Robert A. Baron, he proposed further laboratory experiments which he believed would answer some of the questions raised by critics of his (and others') earlier experiments. He was given a contract of $13,000.

Among the critics of experiments, such as those Liebert and Bandura had performed, was Dr. Joseph Klapper, Director of Research for CBS Television. In his testimony before the Media Task Force of the Eisenhower Commission in 1968, and in books on the subject, Dr. Klapper expressed doubts about the relationship of televised violence to aggressive behavior. Specifically, he questioned the relationship of laboratory experiments to the everyday world of children. Liebert felt that "among the most important and not unreasonable criticisms [by Klapper] was that Bandura and we had used films constructed in our own laboratories."[19] Liebert considered that a fair criticism, because the real question of concern to the public—and now to the Surgeon General's Advisory Committee—was, "What does commercial television do?" Further, Bandura had used the plastic Bobo clown in his experimental films; Liebert had used adults dressed like Bobo in the films made for his later experiments. Yet no actual television program showed Bobo—whether real or plastic—being pummeled by a person. Liebert acknowledged that "it was of interest to determine whether or not you could instigate aggression, by children against other children, by using regular television programs."[20]

One limitation of laboratory experiments that could not be "corrected" was that a real child could not be used as the specified object of possible aggression. The furthest researchers had gone was to have an adult dressed like Bobo receive blows from children. (One of Liebert's colleagues carried a red mark on her arm for several hours from a youngster's mallet blow.) Some of the experiments included periods of "natural play" when researchers could observe children's attitudes and actions towards other children, as well as towards inanimate objects such as plastic clowns. But it was impermissible to set up a situation in which a child who had been subjected to a film or television sequence containing aggressive actions would then be given the opportunity to imitate those actions against another child. The problem was to try to create a situation that would test a child's willingness to hurt another child without actually involving that child.

One hundred thirty-six children—half of whom were boys and half, girls, divided approximately into five- or six-year-olds and eight- or nine-year-olds—participated in the experiment which Liebert and Baron designed in an effort to overcome such problems. One group of children was allowed to watch a televised program for six-and-one-half minutes, containing two-and-one-half minutes of commercials, and three-and-one-half minutes of a program from "The Untouchables." That sequence was a direct and uncut portion from an actual program featuring a chase, two fist-fights, two shootings, and a knifing. Meanwhile, the children in a control group saw the same commercials, but instead of the violent sequence, witnessed a videotaped sports event with competitions in races, hurdles, and high jumps.

Just before the end of the television sequences, the "experimenter" entered the room and said to a participating child that the experiment in which he or she was going to help was now ready. Ushered into another room, the child was seated before a gray metal response box which had a red button on one side, a green button on the other, and a white light at the top center. Under the red button was the word "Hurt"; under the green button, "Help." The experimenter explained to the child that in an adjacent room, another child was going to play a game which required turning a handle. Each time the other child started to turn the handle, the white light would come on. The experimenter continued:

> When this white light comes on, you have to push one of these two buttons. If you push this green button, that will make the handle next door easier to turn and will help the child to win the game. If you push this red button, that will make the handle next door feel hot. That will hurt the child, and he will have to let go of the handle . . . The longer you push the green button, the more you will help the other child and the longer you push the red button, the more you hurt the other child.[21]

Actually, there was no other child in the adjacent room. But each child in the experiment thought there was and was given twenty opportunities to help or to hurt. The result: The children who saw the violent film sequences subsequently were more likely to act aggressively toward the unseen child than were those who viewed the neutral film. "Further," the researchers noted, "the present results emerged despite the brevity of the aggressive sequences (less than four minutes), the absence of a strong prior instigation to aggression, and the clear availability of an alternative helping response."[22]

In the Liebert and Baron study, exposure to only three-and-one-half minutes of a violent television sequence caused children from five to nine years old to behave more aggressively immediately afterwards. Given most children's regular viewing habits, the question becomes whether constant exposure to televised violence over long periods of time produces equally predictable and undesirable results. That was one of the questions which the Fels Institute team recognized was still not answered as it completed its experiment.

Working with the filming of children in the Liebert-Baron experiment—in a collaborative effort the Advisory Committee staff had encouraged—a research team from the University of California at San Francisco pinpointed a factor which seemed to predict "post-viewing" activities and actions. The team was led by Professor Paul Eckman, a psychologist pioneering in the study of facial expressions and their meanings. Eckman's previous research on adults had showed that facial expressions were a reliable measure of the kind of stimuli the person had been subjected to; in his experiment, the question was whether children's emotional reactions as revealed by facial expressions while watching violent television material might predict the incidence of subsequent aggressive behavior.

The hypothesis of the UCSF researchers was this: children registering expressions of happiness, pleasantness, and interest while watching violent action on television would be "positively related" to subsequent aggression; expressions of unpleasantness, sadness, fear, disgust, pain, or disinterest would be "negatively related" to subsequent aggression.[23]

The Eckman study involved five- and six-year-olds—thirty boys and thirty-five girls. They were divided into two groups, "experimental" and "control." Each child watched television alone for about six-and-one-half minutes, first viewing two one-minute commercials (which had actually been broadcast in 1970). The commercials included a number of sudden events which the researchers thought were sufficient to provide a basis for evaluating the child's facial "responsivity." Subsequently, the children in the experimental group saw the sequence from "The Untouchables" and those in the control group saw the sports sequence, both previously described.

Liebert and Baron in their study examined the relationship between the two types of television sequence and the children's subsequent aggressive or non-aggressive actions. To evaluate the third factor, Professor Eckman and his colleagues used the following technique:

> A videotape recording of each child's face was made during the entire period the child was in the television room. None of the children included in the data analysis noticed the camera, which was in another room and aimed through a small pane of clear glass. The videorecording also included a multiplexed small image of the television program the child was watching.

The sound track of the television program and any sounds made by the child were recorded on the audio track of the videotape.[24]

Later, eight groups of "judges"—all specially instructed college undergraduates—viewed tapes of the children's reactions (but not the films they had been shown) and judged the emotion registered in their faces according to one of two forms:

One form asked the observers to record their judgments on each of four nine-point scales labeled *pleasant-unpleasant, interested-disinterested, aroused-unaroused,* and *involved-uninvolved.* The other form asked the observers to rate each of the following emotions: *anger, happiness, disgust, fear, pain, sadness,* and *surprise,* using a nine-point scale to record whether each emotion was absent or slightly, moderately, or extremely shown.[25]

The pooled judgments were combined and coded. Then, their findings were compared with the results of the "Hurt-Help" tests of those children administered by Liebert and Baron.

The results for the young boys supported the hypothesis being tested. Those boys whose faces showed pleasure or happiness when viewing the violent films were much more apt to push the "Hurt" button. And the stronger their pleasurable reaction to violence, the quicker and longer they pushed the "Hurt" button. Conversely, the boys who showed feelings of disinterest, unhappiness, or displeasure to the violent sequences were significantly more likely to "Help" rather than "Hurt." No correlation between visible emotions and aggressiveness was found for the boys who viewed the nonviolent television sequence. However, an unexpected finding was revealed: There were no consistent correlations for either violent or nonviolent viewing among the girls.

Dr. Eckman and his colleagues cautioned that their research could not be considered definitive without further verification. In particular, they urged further research to answer questions about the girls' responses, and about *why* some boys reacted with pleasure and interest, while others reacted with sadness and disinterest to shooting or fighting. But the researchers had provided another link of evidence about the relationship between television violence and aggressive behavior. In their words:

These findings for the boys suggest that, in order to understand the influence of televised violence on the likelihood of subsequent aggression, we must consider the child's emotional reaction to the violence. . . . This study has shown that there are markedly different emotional reactions to the same violent program and that these different reactions, as indicated by facial expression, *do* predict subsequent aggression.[26]

Professor Bradley Greenberg, of Michigan State University, reviewing the laboratory experiments for the Advisory Committee, agreed that the Eckman study needed follow-up. For one thing, he thought it imperative that comparable analyses be made of the older boys—the eight- and nine-year-olds—that Liebert and Baron had tested. But Greenberg thought that the correlation the Eckman team found between young boys' facial expressions and their subsequent aggressive actions was "rather striking."[27]

These and other new laboratory experiments thus advanced understanding of whether violence viewing might be associated with aggressiveness. Other experiments advanced knowledge in another way: by producing results which appeared to refute a previous thesis. This thesis, often cited by broadcasters, was that television violence acted as a cathartic agent, helping aggressive children, adolescents, and adults vicariously relieve themselves of hostile emotions. It was based in large part on the earlier work of Dr. Seymour Feshbach of the University of California at Los Angeles. His studies of adolescent and pre-adolescent boys, reported to the Eisenhower Commission, led him to conclude that, at least under some circumstances, television violence viewing did have a "cathartic effect" on youngsters.

Feshbach believed that one of the strengths of his research was that it was performed "in a naturalistic setting." The setting for his earlier project was a series of boys' schools—three private schools and four homes for boys of low socioeconomic background whose families were unable to take care of them. Over a six-week period, 665 boys ranging in age from ten to seventeen "were randomly assigned within each institution either to a television schedule containing predominantly aggressive programs or to a control treatment of predominantly nonaggressive programs."[28] Adult supervisors in each school recorded and rated the boys' behavior according to a formal questionnaire developed by Dr. Feshbach. Analyzing his data, Feshbach reported:

> The most impressive differences were yielded by the behavior ratings, which essentially recorded aggressive incidents. The frequency of verbal

aggression and physical aggression, whether directed toward peers or toward authority figures, was consistently higher in the control group exposed to the nonaggressive programs than in the experimental group placed on the aggressive "diet."[29]

Critics of Dr. Feshbach's experiment claimed that the setting was so special—and the subjects so unrepresentative a sample of American boys—that even if the findings reported for that sample were sound, they were not necessarily applicable to the real world.

But, because of these claims and counterclaims, considerable attention was given to the catharsis theory by the Surgeon General's Advisory Committee. Dr. Liebert was asked to review and comment upon Feshbach's earlier experiment. Others attempted to test the catharsis theory in their own research.

Liebert and two colleagues, examining Feshbach's earlier study, found "four potentially crippling weaknesses."[30] First, in the study of those schoolboys in homes, the investigators had used a behavior rating scale that had not been "scientifically established." Second, the assignment of some boys to the control group watching exclusively nonaggressive programs—despite their possible preferences for other kinds of programs—might have led to frustration or resentment that made them behave more aggressively. Third, some of those in the control group were also permitted to watch their favorite "aggressive" programs as well as the prescribed "nonaggressive" fare. Fourth, the raters were "cottage supervisors" and others untrained in performing the required tasks, and their own relationships with the boys—their biases or expectations—might have affected the way they rated the boys' aggressiveness.[31]

Feshbach replied that his critics had "ignored a great deal of relevant data"[32] and suggested a bias in their own attitudes that showed in their critiques. Liebert and his colleagues, wrote Feshbach in the jargon of social science disputation, "convey theoretical and methodological orientations which we do not share."[33] But the preponderance of the research commissioned by the Surgeon General's Committee failed to sustain Feshbach. According to Committee member Ithiel de Sola Pool's testimony, the catharsis thesis could now be discarded. Even Joseph Klapper seemed willing to discard this thesis. As he testified before the Committee, "I myself am unaware of any, shall we say hard evidence that seeing violence on television or any other medium acts in a cathartic or subliminated manner." Studies such as Feshbach's, he added, were "grossly, greatly outweighed" by studies supporting the opposite conclusion.[34]

Some of the new laboratory experiments advanced understanding by providing new evidence; some effectively eliminated previous hypotheses; still others resulted in no substantive findings. One significant experiment enlarged the context in which the issue of televised violence and aggressive action would have to be considered. Professor Percy Tannenbaum of the University of California at Berkeley launched a major project to test the hypothesis of whether "heightened arousal," regardless of the type of program content producing it, led to more "responsiveness," including aggressive actions. Dr. Tannenbaum's study, one of the largest supported by the Television and Social Behavior Program, lasted several years—the only one funded beyond the Surgeon General's Committee time span. In a series of experiments under this project, Tannenbaum varied the message content and the conditions under which the films were shown. A variety of subjects was used, but in all the experiments reported so far they were exclusively junior high school students.[35]

The basic experimental design of Tannenbaum's studies was as follows:

> First, there is an encounter between a subject and an experimenter (or his confederate), in which the subject is angered. This has been done in two ways: (1) where testing is with one subject at a time, the anger is induced through a series of mild electric shocks; (2) in group testing, the subjects are grossly insulted by a substitute teacher.[36]

After this "pre-conditioning," the subjects view films designed to offer different kinds of stimuli. Tannenbaum varied the message content of the film sequences: either erotic, violent, or neutral. Following exposure to the film stimulus, various response situations were established for the subject, singly and in groups. Each was given a chance to administer electric shocks to others; alternatively, each was allowed to "rate" the competence of the "substitute teacher" and recommend whether that teacher should be offered a regular teaching position. Additional measures were made of the boys' and girls' state of arousal and the nature or form of the outlets of that arousal.[37]

If Tannenbaum's findings are sustained, they add important

qualifications to the effects of television viewing: erotic arousal may be more intensively linked to subsequent aggressive behavior than violent arousal. Suggestive violence on the screen may be more arousing than explicit violence. In his progress report for the Advisory Committee, Tannenbaum could only conclude on the basis of his work up to that point that arousal clearly produces more active behavior, and that "cognitive message cues, like the aggression in violent content, may interact with generalized arousal to contribute to even higher levels of aggression than arousal itself might produce."[38]

As Tannenbaum continued his work, others urged that this line of research be extended to a population of younger viewers. For, as Dr. Greenberg commented, "If youngsters are more easily aroused, or aroused to a greater degree [than older adolescents] by the same stimuli, the subsequent behaviors should be more intense."[39]

It is not surprising, but it is significant that almost all the hypotheses tested or questions posed in new research efforts were subsequently judged to need further exploration. This was even true in the case of experiments which yielded no evidence in support of the validity of the questions being explored. For example, one research effort sought to determine the usefulness of dream content as an index of certain viewer reaction to television violence.[40] Earlier research had resulted in contradictory findings. The new study was carefully controlled, yet the researchers were forced to conclude:

> The findings of the present study indicate that the violent film did not have any systematic effect on dream hostility, anxiety, guilt, hedonic tone, or overall vividness and intensity. They thus are in direct agreement with the results of neither of the earlier two studies relating media violence to dream content.[41]

Professor Greenberg commented in his review for the Surgeon General's Committee:

> When faced with three different sets of findings from three different experiments in a continuing research program, and when the most recent test is the most precise and carefully executed, one is tempted to give up on dreams as a path to the understanding of media effects on aggressiveness.[42]

Still, Greenberg felt obliged to suggest that further study might be "very valuable."

Attempting to measure social behavior in the laboratory is not without its critics, even among the social scientists. James Q. Wilson, the Harvard political scientist, has ridiculed the notion that experiments of the type described here have relevance to a real life setting. He critiques Bandura's use of Bobo dolls: "Bandura argues that his definition of 'aggression'—performing certain kinds of physical acts, such as hitting or kicking—is appropriate even though it is directed at nonhuman objects, but it is hard to imagine why it *should* be appropriate unless one can show that harmless play activity will be transferred to interpersonal situations. But this is precisely what has not been shown."[43] Wilson similarly challenges the tests in which the child is measured for aggression by the way he administers electric shocks to a fictional counterpart.

Percy Tannenbaum argues in reply:

> The charge is made that we don't have good measures. But in experimental research, we use the same inadequate measure under the same conditions except the condition that the experimenter has varied systematically—in this case, the kind of film or TV show the kids have been exposed to. So if there are differences, what you want to account for is those differences. It's not adequate to say the measure wasn't good enough. Once you've accepted, say, that pseudo-electric shocks or how many times you kick the Bobo doll is going to be used for the purposes of this study as an adequate measure of the term "aggression," then *what the statistics are about is the difference between the groups.*
>
> When there is random behavior among the kids in my lab toward what buttons they push, there is the same chance of equally random behavior whether they saw an aggressive movie or a non-aggressive movie. If there are differences in the "mean" and around the "mean" in each group—greater than the differences among the children *within* a group—then we say that is a significant finding. It could have occurred by chance in only a small percentage of the cases.
>
> I am dissatisfied that we measure aggression in different ways. But I am impressed when different investigators do indeed measure the relationship between TV viewing and aggressive behavior in different ways—each with its own flaws but each with its own rationale as well—and they come up with similar findings. That is impressive because the differences should contribute to a lower relationship, not a higher one. It gives increased validity to the random nature of the research projects.[44]

How much further can laboratory experimentation be pushed? The question raises unavoidable problems, not the least being the severe limitations placed on using human beings as guinea pigs. Now that the Surgeon General's Committee has issued its findings, there will be even greater caution about stimulating test groups of children to potentially aggressive behavior.

The battle over the validity of the social science laboratory may be unending. Possibly the greatest significance of the lab experiments performed for the Surgeon General's Committee was that in the main they reinforced evidence collected in the field. It is to these field studies that we now must turn.

5

WHAT THE RESEARCHERS FOUND: IN THE FIELD

"Field studies," which constituted the second major group of projects supported by the Television and Social Behavior Program, encompassed an even greater variety of research approaches than the laboratory studies. There were both "experimental" studies, similar to the laboratory tests but conducted in real-life settings, and "correlational" studies in which various kinds of data were systematically analyzed to see which factors—such as television violence viewing and aggressive behavior—were closely related.*

The most glaring gap in earlier work had been the lack of adequate measurements of children's television habits over extended periods of time. By sheer accident, an opportunity presented itself to the Advisory Committee which went a long way toward filling that gap.

---

*The Surgeon General's Advisory Committee had hoped to sponsor the ultimate in field studies: a comparative study in a fairly large city in "middle America" whose cable television system would permit the broadcasting of different programs (for at least a few hours per day) to two sample groups of a large homogeneous population. One such community in West Virginia was singled out. But there were major control problems connected with this project. Also, it would cost no less than $250,000—one-fourth of the entire research budget. In the end, it was decided that the study would be too difficult, too uncertain, and too costly.

In 1955, Dr. Leonard Eron, head of research for the Rip Van Winkle Foundation, began examining the prevalence of mental health problems in Columbia County, a rural area in upstate New York. To make sure that their observations would be reliable and relevant, Dr. Eron and his colleagues chose a single indicator of mental and emotional problems which they believed could be measured objectively: aggression. Their definition of aggression, refined in the early stages of their study, was: a punitive act which injures or irritates another person.[1]

Rather than try to select a balanced, representative smaller sample of children, the researchers decided to study all children in the third grade in Columbia County. Most of the children were eight years old. At that age, they were able to write the simple answers the questions required. Further, earlier research had demonstrated that by the age of eight, children have probably developed stable patterns of behavior. Thus, the findings of Eron and his colleagues would better serve as a base line against which the children's future behavior could be compared.

In addition to securing responses of the children about themselves, the researchers sought data about each child from four other sources: his classmates, his mother, his father, and his teacher. Dr. Eron and his colleagues wanted to determine whether different levels of aggressiveness among the children they worked with could be traced to familial, social, economic, geographic, and/or cultural factors. A second goal was to gain an understanding of the learning conditions for aggression.[2] For example, what kinds of values do parents convey to children about using aggressive actions, and how does this influence the way children act out their aggressive instincts?

One of the most important things the researchers wanted to study was the consistency over time of aggressive behavior of the Columbia County children. Their plan was to follow up the third grade survey when the children reached the eighth grade, and again when they reached the twelfth grade. The researchers planned to study the children for nine years to test the theory that patterns of behavior remain consistent over time, hence childhood behavior may predict adolescent and adult behavior.

The researchers collected information from 875 children about themselves and their classmates. The children were asked which of their classmates behaved aggressively in the classroom. Examples: "Who (among your classmates) starts a fight over nothing?" "Who is always getting into trouble?" "Who says mean things?" Other questions elicited information on popularity, aggression, anxiety, success in aggression, masculine-feminine identification, and occupational aspirations. IQ's were taken from school records. Mothers and fathers were asked how frequently their children watched television and what types of programs they watched. They were also asked about the child's reading of comic books, their own familiarity with Dr. Spock's book on child care, and other matters relating to the home and family environment.[3]

Later, when interest grew in the effect of television on behavior, the researchers went back to their data and analyzed the relationship between the child's favorite television programs (as reported by parents), the violence content of those programs, and the child's "aggression rating" provided by classmates. They found "a significant positive relationship . . . among boys between television violence and peer ratings of aggression";[4] among girls, the relationship between these factors was less strong though in the same direction.

The study had its critics. Both a local newspaper and the American Legion Post accused the researchers, as well as the Rip Van Winkle Foundation and the local school board, of a host of sins from invasion of privacy (because of the "personal questions" in the questionnaires) to promotion of the "mental health movement" as a weapon "to bring about conformity to the Marxist ideology."[5] The researchers won that battle, so the first segment of the study was completed. But local suspicions remained.

Important though this research turned out to be, it was apparently not considered particularly important at the time. The NIMH declined to renew support for the project in 1962, and again in 1964 rejected a request for support. In 1968, the research team applied to HEW's Office of Crime and Delinquency for a grant, and was turned down.[6]

Despite his problems, and because of what he believed to be the importance of the long-range effort, Dr. Monroe Lefkowitz of New York State's Department of Mental Hygiene fought to keep the project alive. With the help of the original research team, Dr. Eron, Dr. Leopold Walder, and a statistician, Dr. L. Rowell Huesmann, a limited effort was made to test the children when they reached the eighth grade. Unable to secure funding, the research team later reported that it "confined itself to those schools most readily accessible and to a circumscribed number of subjects." Three hundred eighty-two children were tested, but only 252 of them had been in the original third-grade population. Dr. Walder subsequently commented to Senator Pastore on the government's lack of interest in the project in the early part of the decade:

> Now, these kinds of studies are very rarely funded by NIMH or by the government in general, because the payoff is slow in coming. The administration that says we let out a grant today cannot show results until perhaps many years later.[7]

The greatly reduced sample seriously weakened the eighth-grade follow-up, but fortunately it kept the research team aware of the potential their two efforts represented. Having become interested in the television factor as a possibly important indicator of aggressive behavior, they made a study of relevant data on third-graders in Alexandria, Virginia. The investigators found "a statistically significant relation" between viewing television violence and reported aggression. As in the case of the Columbia County third-graders, the greater amount of television violence viewed, the higher were the peer ratings of aggression.[8]

When plans for the Surgeon General's Advisory Committee were announced in the spring of 1969, Dr. Lefkowitz arranged a quick, preliminary survey of Columbia County high school graduates of that year. At least 52 percent of the original subject pool was still in the county. The possibility of capturing data already recorded and extending the earlier research into a longitudinal study keenly interested the Surgeon General's Advisory Committee and its staff. A grant of $42,000 was awarded Dr. Lefkowitz (who was designated chief investigator) and his colleagues. Between June and October, 1970, the research team was able to conduct personal interviews with 436 of the original 875 subjects first tested in the third grade.

These nineteen-year-olds were asked the same questions about their classmates that they had been asked ten years earlier. In addition to repeating questions on nine "aggression" items, the questionnaire contained other items relating to anxiety, popularity, activity level, and leadership.[9]

In this ten-year follow-up study, the recently graduated students were asked to name their current four favorite programs. As before, two independent raters designated the programs as violent or nonviolent, and once again there was high agreement on the ratings.[10] If there is dispute over what televised violence does, there is little disagreement about what violence looks like.

During the course of the three stages of the longitudinal study, the investigators collected information in six categories from the subjects, their peers, their mothers, and their fathers. The categories were aggression, social status, psychopathology, television use, height, and school records. Data were collected on specific variables (measurable characteristics) in each category. For example, under social status, information was taken on the occupation of the father, the number of books in the home, the father's and mother's education, and the father's and mother's aspirations for their child. In all, the research team collected information on ninety-four variables.

Examining those variables, the investigators found a strong correlation between early television violence viewing and aggressive behavior in the teenage years. The relationship was found to be even stronger than that between television viewing and aggressive behavior in the third grade.[11] The cross-lagged correlation—the linking of variables existing at one particular time with those existing at later or earlier times—was a distinctive feature of this study.

Social scientists recognize that a strong, regularly found correlation between two variables means that each can be "predicted" from the other statistically. They caution, however, that such statistical correlations do not prove that one variable is the cause of the other. It might simply be that the children who were more inclined to be aggressive toward others were also more likely to enjoy watching aggressive actions on television. This possibility could be considered a "rival hypothesis" to the notion that watching television violence *causes* aggressive behavior.

In the longitudinal study, however, correlations between television violence and aggressive behavior could be measured four ways. The four variables include 1) aggressiveness at age eight, 2) televised violence viewing at age eight, 3) aggressiveness at age nineteen, and 4) televised violence viewing at age nineteen. Thus, Drs. Lefkowitz, Eron, Walder and Huesmann concluded:

[P]reference for a violent television diet in the third grade leads to aggressive behavior at that time and also in late adolescence.[12]

According to their study, a child's television habits at age eight are more likely to be a predictor of his aggressiveness at age eighteen or nineteen than his family's socioeconomic status, his relationships with his parents, his IQ, or any other single factor in his environment. Only one factor is as good a predictor: if the child is aggressive at age eight, he is likely to be aggressive at age eighteen or nineteen. And since viewing televised violence at age eight is also related to aggressiveness at that age, Dr. Lefkowitz and his colleagues reached the conclusion:

> On the basis of these cross-lagged correlations, the most plausible single causal hypothesis would appear to be that preferring violent television fare in the third grade leads to the building of aggressive habits.[13]

In a further search for experimental field research, Dr. Rubinstein found "an extremely well designed study" which was proposed by two faculty members of Pennsylvania State University's Division of Individual and Family Studies. The design was especially important because its goal was ambitious and the researchers were relatively unknown.

Drs. Aletha Stein and Lynette Friedrich proposed to compare the effects of television programs on the behavior of preschool children in a naturalistic setting.[14] Awarded a contract, they and a team of graduate students looked closely at the daily behavior of ninety-seven nursery school children over a period of nine weeks. For the first three weeks the researchers simply observed the children in their regular class and play activities; this was to make sure that the observers were reliable and consistent in what they observed and recorded and to establish each child's ordinary behavior patterns. During the next four weeks, the children were divided into three groups. Each group regularly viewed one of three series of short television film episodes. One series emphasized the aggressive condition and included six "Batman" and six "Superman" cartoons. A second series contained "neutral" programming and included children's films which had neither aggressive nor prosocial content. The third series featured prosocial content— twelve episodes from "Mister Rogers' Neighborhood" with themes of sharing, cooperative behavior, and self-discipline.[15] Observations were continued during a two-week postviewing period during which no television was shown.

The observers recorded information about each child according to six stimulus categories and sixteen behavior categories. In the former group were such items as frustration provoked by another child or by a situation difficult for the child to cope with. Among behavior categories were physical and verbal aggression, cooperation, rule obedience, tolerance of delay, and task persistence.[16]

A central finding was:

> [C]hildren who were initially high in aggression showed greater interpersonal aggression when they were exposed to the Aggressive condition than when they were exposed to the Neutral or Prosocial conditions.[17]

The investigators noted on the other hand that "children who were initially low in aggression"—as observed in the first three weeks of nursery school—"did not respond differentially to the television conditions."[18] Equally important was the finding that "the clearest main effects of the television programs appeared on the self-controlling behaviors. Children exposed to the prosocial television programs showed higher levels of rule obedience, tolerance of delay, and persistence than children exposed to the aggressive programs."[19]

There were qualifications to these findings: Children with higher IQ's responded to the "lessons" of self-control and task persistence. Children from low socioeconomic backgrounds responded more noticeably to themes of cooperation. "It is particularly interesting to note this response," the researchers commented, "as critics have frequently suggested that the appeal of the program ('Mister Rogers' Neighborhood') was limited to middle-class children."[20]

More confusing, at least to the layman, was the Stein–Friedrich finding that:

> At the same time, self-controlling behavior—particularly tolerance for minor frustrations—declined for all children exposed to the aggressive condition. This reduction in self-control was accompanied, for higher SES [socio-economic status] children, by increased social interaction that was primarily cooperative. It appears, therefore, that the aggressive programs had a general stimulating effect for the higher SES children that led to higher

social interaction and lower levels of personal control. For those who were already aggressive, it led to aggression as well.[21]

Weighing the implications of their findings, the researchers concluded:

> Television critics have frequently pointed out the one-sided nature of current viewing fare. Violent solutions to problems, whether by villain or hero, have been standard in an endless series of programs. . . . Such viewing has an impact not only on aggressive behavior, but also on other aspects of behavior like self-control.
>
> But the equally important implications which can be drawn from the data are those that support the belief that television can play an important role in the positive social development of children.[22]

Data collected over a year were used in several related studies by Professors Steven Chaffee, Jack McLeod, and Charles Atkins of the University of Wisconsin. They tried to test the relationships among three sets of variables: 1) adolescent aggression; 2) television viewing; and 3) structural attributes of family social environment.[23] In essence, their focus on family environment was an attempt to pinpoint the home conditions under which television violence viewing might contribute to aggressive tendencies and actions.

The data were usually collected in two ways. For example, in a study of 225 adolescents in Wisconsin, a group of sixth graders and a group of ninth graders were asked to fill out questionnaires regarding their viewing habits and preferences and their attitudes and likely actions in various situations, both hypothetical and actual. At the same time, their mothers were interviewed, as were some of their friends and teachers. A year later, with one group now in the seventh grade and the other in the tenth grade, new questionnaires and additional maternal interviews were completed.[24]

Like all other researchers, McLeod, Atkins, and Chaffee first had to define aggression. (Such definitions varied considerably among the studies. Although some authorities criticized the variance, members of the Surgeon General's Advisory Committee thought it strengthened the overall research results.) The Wisconsin group devised a twenty-item index, with several subheadings: assault aggression, verbal aggression, irritability, approval of aggression, and aggressive attitudes. The parts added up to what the researchers called "the overall aggression sum."[25]

In measuring family environment, the researchers gathered data on a number of elements including: parental emphasis on nonaggression; parental interpretation of violence; punishment; affection; and family communications patterns.[26]

The Wisconsin researchers did not summarize their conclusions, but the following is a paraphrase of their several findings:

1. Overall violence viewing has a positive correlation with aggressive actions as reported by the children and others.
2. There is a stronger relationship between specific violence viewing and aggression, than between general television viewing and aggression.
3. Past violence viewing is also related to aggressive behavior, a finding that questions the hypothesis that aggressive behavior results in violence viewing rather than vice versa.
4. Virtually all indices of aggression, violence viewing, and cognitive reaction decline between the junior high and senior high school years.
5. Adolescents who perform poorly in school watch considerably more violent television, are more likely to approve of aggression, and are generally more likely to behave aggressively.
6. Socioeconomic status is not so clear a predictor of violence viewing and aggressive behavior as previous research might have suggested.
7. There seems to be a strong relationship between mothers' and children's behavior—a child's modeling a mother's behavior—in assault aggression, verbal aggression, and approval of aggression.
8. Aggression modeling is greater for mother–daughter than for mother–son pairs.
9. There is also reverse modeling in television viewing patterns: Parents are as likely to watch television programs favored by their children as vice versa.
10. Parental attempts to influence the child's television behavior by controlling watching and by interpreting violence apparently have little effect.[27]

Two broad implications emerge from the Chaffee–McLeod–Atkins studies. First, the most constant relationships among the three sets of factors examined were between viewing television violence and subsequent aggressive behavior. These two factors had a high correlation when a whole range of other variables were controlled: socioeconomic status, age, sex, regional differences, and overall amount of general television viewing time. Second, although some family environmental variables relate to violence viewing and aggressive behavior, few seemed to be strong enough to counteract the correlation between high violence viewing and aggressive activities on the part of adolescents.[28]

Lest parents think such results mean they can do nothing to affect television's impact on their children, the researchers did offer one recommendation: Parental example—specifically, "the mother's own behavior with respect to aggressiveness"—can be a strong factor in affecting the child's behavior.[29] The Wisconsin professors rejected what they considered indirect or "gatekeeping" parental strategies—limiting a child's intake of television violence[30]—in favor of a "direct strategy" of emphasizing nonaggression to the child.

The mounting evidence generated by the experimental and correlational studies in the field, added to that of controlled laboratory experiments, thus continued to indicate a strong connection between children's viewing of television violence and their subsequent aggressiveness, whether immediately afterwards or years later. Certain aspects of the relationship between television and the child had been pinpointed: Television could be and often was instructional as regards behavior patterns; it could and sometimes did produce children's imitation of behaviors learned; it could in any case affect attitudes, including those about the propriety of aggressiveness; and it could affect attitudes and behaviors in either positive, prosocial ways or in negative, antisocial ways.

Other studies sought to illuminate the nature of the conditions under which children watched television. Dr. Jack Lyle summed up six research efforts which showed that "children's viewing of television is likely to be far from passive" and equally likely to be far from exclusive. In his own study—a follow-up to the landmark effort he undertook with Wilbur Schramm and Edwin Parker ten years before—Lyle found that more than 80 percent of the first graders in his sample said they engaged in other activities such as eating, playing, and talking, while viewing television.[31] Others found that 1) attention declined as programs progressed;

2) students studied while watching; 3) most children and adults viewed television with others and engaged in conversation while watching. In short, rarely do viewers give the television set full attention.

The most interesting new evidence in this area came from a study conducted by Robert Bechtel, Clark Achelpohl, and Roger Akers, of the Greater Kansas City Mental Health Foundation.[32] After interviewing several dozen families about their viewing habits, these researchers obtained permission from a few of them to install cameras in their homes. The researchers found, first, that the interviewees had considerably over-reported their viewing time; in fact, they did not actually view as many programs as they said they did. Second, the film tapes made by the cameras proved that even with sets turned on, home viewers actually "watched" the television only 55 to 76 percent of the time the program was on the air. Reporting on a family of four who were supposed to be viewing "I Love Lucy" together, the investigators found at least one parent or one of the two children out of the room at all times. They listed some of the activities the four engaged in while "Lucy" was on: looking out window; scratching (someone else and self); rocking; reading; clearing table; undressing; whistling; scolding children; mimicking the television; eating; conversing; using phone; playing with dog; asking questions about the television program; combing hair. Bechtel and his associates cautioned that "no conclusions can be drawn from this one record."[33] But, they said, it was not atypical of the results of their 613 tapes of watching-nonwatching patterns.

Asked to comment on the fear expressed by some laymen and social commentators that television is turning America's young into a generation of passive vegetables, one researcher replied: "Anybody who thinks that has never watched children watch TV."

The exact nature of the relationship of television and the child remained open to question. Perhaps the sheer persistence of the medium—its ubiquitous presence and the heavy dosages of violence it offers—made the difference. Regardless of the exact psychological and sociological processes involved, the new research heightened the realization that television was a powerful instrument for affecting the interest, feelings, attitudes, beliefs, and behavior of its viewers. As we will see in the next chapter, the investigators also discovered that television powerfully affects those who participate in it from the other side—the writers, producers, executives, and others to whom the questions raised by Senator Pastore had to be addressed.

6

WHAT THE RESEARCHERS FOUND: IN THE INDUSTRY AND ON THE AIR

While others continued to explore and debate the effect of televised violence on the nation's children, both George Gerbner, of the Annenberg School of Communications at the University of Pennsylvania, and David G. Clark and William B. Blankenburg, of the University of Wisconsin, were conducting surveys to ascertain the amount and character of this violence. Using a content-analysis approach to chart long-term trends, these studies substantiated the belief that violent action is the main staple of television fare. By analyzing in detail the number of violent incidents during one week of fall prime-time and Saturday morning programming in 1969 and comparing the results with similar analyses for 1967 and 1968, Gerbner's study showed that violence was persisting despite professed efforts to reduce it.[1] Although lethal violence dropped sharply and the proportion of leading characters involved in violence dropped over this three-year period, the rate of violent incidents on television as a whole continued steady, and violence in children's cartoons increased markedly.

Using similar statistical methods, Clark and Blankenburg's study further showed that violent programs followed a cyclical pattern having no connection with violence patterns of the real world. Instead, violence appeared to vary in accordance with indexes of its popularity. Despite the repeated concern expressed by both Congress and citizens' groups, high ratings for violent programs in one season proved to be major determinants for the number of violent programs the next season. Clark and Blankenburg found that this rising pattern of violence appeared to peak every four years.[2]

In order to get a better perspective on why this kind of programming is such an enduring phenomenon, Professors Thomas F. Baldwin and Colby Lewis of the department of television and radio at Michigan State University conducted a study examining violence from the broadcast industry's point of view. Specifically, Baldwin and Lewis wanted to determine the television industry's: own beliefs about why violence is a persistent ingredient in popular television drama; awareness of its youth audience; perceptions of the effects of violence both on children and on the general audience; and judgment of just where responsibility for such programming rests.[3]

During the spring of 1970, the two professors began their study by first identifying the network television entertainment series in production for the 1970–71 season that most likely would contain violent acts. Series carried over from the previous season were rated for their violence potential both by a general sample of viewers and by forty-three newspaper and magazine television critics; new series were analyzed on the basis of network promotional material and program descriptions provided by advertising agency personnel who had seen pilots or outlines. The eighteen programs finally selected included all the prime-time commercial network Western, police, detective, and spy series on the air at the beginning of the 1970–71 season. The list did not include newscasts, documentaries, specials, feature films, comedies, variety shows, and general drama. It also excluded programs especially designed for children or long-run syndicated programs which would be less likely to reflect current practice and values.

The second step of the survey was to interview the key person responsible for the content of each listed program—the producer with day-to-day working control and general policy responsibility —as well as writers and others involved in the production process. Equipped with the violence ratings they had compiled and an interview outline which allowed them and the respondents maximum freedom to follow conversational flow, Baldwin and Lewis talked to a total of forty-eight individuals, including ten executive producers, thirteen producers, thirteen writers, four directors, one post-production chief, one columnist, and six network censors.

All of the interviews were conducted in the Los Angeles area between June 21 and July 20, 1970. Both professors participated in the majority of the interviews, which lasted from one to four hours; notes were transcribed by one researcher within a few hours after each session and reviewed by the other. Participants were promised anonymity to encourage candid responses. The report on the interviews presented to the Surgeon General's Committee was neither statistical nor interpretive. Professors Baldwin and Lewis were meticulous about withholding their personal feelings and interpretations. However, as a summary and series of quotations from the interviews, their report provides a comprehensive perspective of the industry's own attitudes toward the violence carried on its programs. It illuminates both the attitudes of those responsible for content and the variety of constraints under which they must function. Two conclusions stand out. First, within the present context of commercial broadcasting, violence is an economic and dramatic imperative that, despite continually changing programming, remains a constant criterion for all thinking and action. Second, the different groups within the industry offer conflicting explanations of just who and what accounts for violent programming.

To television writers, directors, and producers, violence is a fact of life, even though they tend to think in terms of "conflict" and "action beat" rather than "violence" or "aggression."[4] Any decision to be made concerning violence revolves around its degree and quality rather than whether or not it is a suitable action. Program creators refuse to believe that every exhibition of physical force can be construed as violent. Rather, violence is considered excessive only when it is unwarranted. To defend oneself forcefully when attacked and to use force when enemies of society cannot be apprehended by peaceful means is not considered an excessive exertion of physical power.

Producers are quick to point out that violence is in the mainstream of American morality. As an integral part of the truth of life, it cannot be eradicated; for television to gloss it over would result in the medium's losing credibility. Generally, violence is viewed as a relative concept, depending on context—"what the act means to the beholder"[5]—and style of presentation. Producers are resentful of the fact that public disapproval focused on the "happy mayhem of folk violence" in Westerns while the "calculated, sanctified violence of South Viet Nam" continued. As one interviewee asked:

> Before we lay all the blame on TV, how do we explain the actual violence —the use of napalm, for instance—that we condone? If it's fact, seemingly it's not violent. If it's fiction, it is violent.[6]

Program creators feel that dramatic imperatives make violence inevitable. Conflict has always been an ingredient in the drama of the Bible, mythology, folk tales, and epics. Good drama is based on conflict which erupts into violent emotion. Producers further believe that violence is necessary because the reception conditions under which people view television reduce their ability to concentrate. Since programs are viewed with only partial attention, they must be free of "intellect-taxing analyses of life's complex phenomena."[7] Given these conditions, action is the best attention-getter. According to one producer:

> There'll always be a market for action drama on TV. Television is viewed with only part of your attention. Therefore, the style of a television drama has to be simpler, less involved, more forceful. It cannot be subtle. This is not a matter of audience intelligence, but because the conditions under which people view television reduce their acuity and discrimination.[8]

Another producer whose police show attracted forty million viewers stated more simply, "If the show changed to a non-action show, it would begin to fail; so violent action is necessary."[9]

To the producer, audience appeal is also increased by strong contrasts between characters which maximize the possibility of their dynamic interaction and strip them of irrelevant details; by clear-cut, exaggerated attributions of good and evil which allow viewers to identify with the winning side more easily; and by physical jeopardy which is easy to recognize and maintains excitement. All these dramatic dictates are most easily fulfilled through the depiction of violence.

Beyond dramatic imperatives, producers also felt that the individual psyches of their viewers demand violence. Audiences seem more responsive to sensory stimuli which activate the basic biological drives of sex, aggression, and defense. A common technique in escape drama is to work up the spectator's desires, his anticipation, his uncertainty, until these emotions generate a tremendous potential charge which demands release. His satisfaction at the end of the program often depends on the high "voltage" of this charge and the suddenness of its release.

> There must ultimately be some kind of physical settlement. The audience doesn't *see* a jail sentence. It will feel emotionally cheated and complain, "Christ, what a dead ending that was!"[10]

Moreover, producers asserted that to leave the viewer with only the suggestion of violence may have a more adverse effect than complete portrayal because these circumventions suggest the possibility of more violent effects than were actually intended—especially to the fertile imaginations of children.[11]

Striking a balance between intimations of violence and its graphic portrayal is a point of controversy among both producers and critics. During the interviews, some of them pointed out that by underplaying the painful results of violence, it tends to become sanitized, even glamorized. Since television violence is quick and clean, children do not become aware of the agonies such violent behavior produces. However, although a few programmers would make the pain of violence more realistic if they were allowed to, the majority feel that a display of its specific effects would simply be bad television.

> As escape, television can carry realism only so far. The characters on a police show are rough and tough, but they can't show the public the way the job is really done, which would make *The Wild Bunch* look like a Sunday school picnic. If you showed the public that, you wouldn't be making escape entertainment; you'd be telling them there isn't a Santa Claus.[12]

Producers stated that there was no place on television for the kind of violence which their audiences would consider repugnant, which would leave child spectators emotionally disturbed or which would instruct people in the manufacture and use of unusual weapons. Showing the less immediate and physical consequences of violence—compassion for victims, remorse, grief—is more acceptable and better drama.

Finally, producers pointed out that violence is an economic imperative—the inescapable dictate of the commercial broadcasting system. To the advertiser, violence equals excitement equals ratings. Although a few producers recognized that "it is better business to avoid what others are doing," they generally claimed that competition to win and hold the largest possible audience restrains innovation and accentuates violent content. Material must be progressively stronger in effect in order to maintain the viewer's interest. As one participant observed:

> When the second moon walk was televised, nobody watched. A similar problem confronted the producers of *The Untouchables*. "Last week you killed three men; what are you going to do this week?" So the producers began to lean more heavily on the violence.[13]

Many of those interviewed believed that some demonstration of violence is beneficial. Although they acknowledged that violent programming might trigger the disturbed, they felt that it would be "unfair" to cater to a small minority.[14] For the general public, television might rather have a calming effect by allowing the viewer to vent vicariously his aggressive urges. The more pronounced the stamping out of evil, the more assurance for the viewer that these aggressive tendencies which he fears in others and mistrusts in himself have been exorcised. As one respondent claimed:

> The little guy likes violence of this kind because he so seldom reacts effectively against the sources of his own irritations.[15]

Or as another participant observed:

> Human culture is a thin shield superimposed over a violent core. It's better to crack it fictionally than to see it explode in the streets. Exposure to properly presented conflicts which result in violence acts as a therapeutic release for anger and self-hatred, which are present in almost everybody.[16]

Respondents also felt violent programs had merit as morality plays carrying socially significant information about the bad effects of violence. Moreover, action-adventure heroes serve as appropriate role models. Most of the leads in these programs, from "Gunsmoke" to "Mod Squad," are presented as protectors of society and champions of the underdog who "succeed against all the evil in the world . . . nobly and cleanly, like a quarterback in a football game."[17]

Program creators had definite ideas about how their programming might affect children's perceptions of violence. In their opinion, by doing a responsible and adult job of "telling it as it is," television helps children learn useful lessons and assimilate conventional cultural values about violence. If the national morality teaches children that there are some values worth fighting for and that there are times when you need to defend yourself, then television is only reflecting these national demands. Moreover, fictional violence also helps children prepare for reality beyond the shelter of suburbia. As one programmer said:

> Exposure to violence in childhood is not a bad idea. Maybe there should be a police show for kids. Ghetto children are exposed to violence unknown to other children. Because they have to live with it and it is so hateful, they might be less influenced by it than other kids who haven't encountered it.[18]

In contrast to this attitude, however, producers also argued that both adults and children could perceive the difference between make-believe and reality. It was felt that children develop notions about violence especially from their own experience quite early in life, at which time they also learn the appropriate social sanctions against it. The effects of adult violent programming are further mitigated, so the producers claimed, by the fact that children are not attracted to adult drama, but rather find it "dull and non-relevant." Producers of early evening action-adventures assumed that the child audience would be watching such shows as "Lassie" or "Wild Kingdom." However, Baldwin and Lewis point out that of the eighteen shows they studied, thirteen had audiences of more than two million viewers in the two–eleven age category; eight shows had over three million child viewers in the twelve–seventeen age category.[19]

Just where does responsibility for violent programming rest? Although the producers proclaimed the cathartic benefits of viewing violence, they were not ready to prescribe its use as conscious social policy. Rather they explained that responsibility for the creative composition of a script was so fractionated among the different sections of production that no one individual could claim the work as his own. Writers, producers, directors, and censors alike complained about constraints—standardized program lengths, mechanical placement of commercials, time limits, heavy rate of consumption for dramatic products in television, need to reach the 18–49 married, higher-income viewers, and the easy rewards for imitating what has proven successful.

Many of the respondents placed the major blame for the lack

of innovative programming on the networks. Fear of government reprisals and of losing audiences, affiliates, and advertisers cause decision-makers to shy away from areas of program content that might be offensive. Rather than being concerned with upgrading their product, they package what will sell. When asked whether paying higher fees to writers might improve their scripts, one producer answered:

> Yeah, better maybe—but we wouldn't get anything different, no bigger breathing hole for the human spirit. The network doesn't like to rock the boat, to tamper with what works. The network people aren't creative. The old studio bosses, for all their faults, had some love for filmmaking. But all the network people do is line up the programs on their long table and juggle them against the competition, asking, "What will work best against that?" instead of, "What are *we* going to do?" The network is run by salesmen. It's their business *not* to *love* the process of making a film.[20]

That program creators view the networks as the focus of blame for violent programming is confirmed by a smaller study conducted by Muriel G. Cantor of American University in 1970.[21] Following interviews with twenty-four script writers and producers of programs aimed specifically at children, Professor Cantor concluded that the networks had become the principal arbiters of children's programming partly because they are viewed as the ones who choose and pay for the programs and partly because alternative influences, such as audience feedback, occur only after production is completed. This applies particularly to the mechanics and economics of children's programming. Not one of the producers interviewed believed that he had extensive creative control. Rather they all felt that to remain in production, they had to conform to the directives of the networks. Producers of children's shows rarely considered the effects violence might have on their audience. Although they acknowledged that children are their target, they also acknowledged that it is the networks that must be satisfied first. They left it up to the networks to translate other influences into appropriate decisions.

Program creators felt that censorship was also imposing unreasonable restrictions on their creative expression. Censors can influence a program at any point from its initiation as a story outline to its completion. At each stage—outline, draft, script, revision, rough film, and completed film—written approval and editorial commentary are involved. Approval is always tentative until the finished product is reviewed; however, the pressure to avoid financial loss puts a premium on incorporating censor changes at the earliest possible stage; the exorbitant costs involved also may inhibit the harshness of the censor's later judgment. In turn, although censors argue against self-censorship during the creative process on the grounds that inventiveness and creativity may be hampered, writers still report that they attempt to submit only "acceptable" ideas. It is a curious bargaining process. Frequently, writers consciously include "excessive" violence on the assumption that every script loses some action at the hands of the censors. If you start with what you want, you will end up with less. Therefore, "The easiest way to deal with a censor is to load it [the script] with things you know they'll take out, leaving what you want."[22]

Professors Baldwin and Lewis found little serious concern among censors for the social effects of television violence. Their goal seemed to be to work efficiently in the production process and to avoid criticism from the public, station affiliates, or governmental agencies. As one director explained, "Censors are not basically motivated by any great social conscience. They are motivated, rather, by what will be acceptable."[23]

Industry members were generally hostile toward the outside criticism of television violence. Programmers pointed to the lack of concrete evidence of the negative effects of violence and, although they claimed to keep up with social science research, they refused to acknowledge that it has any practical value for their judgments. They were suspicious of the motives of investigators such as Senator Pastore and claimed that "violence on television is being used as a political tool."[24] Instead, they dramatically pleaded, "let us use the medium to tell the truth, not try to make it acceptable to axe-grinders who use it to further their ends of the moment."[25]

Producers felt that television has become the scapegoat when poverty, racial tension, distrust of government, and alienation should be the true villains. For most people, they asserted, what really influences violent behavior are social norms resulting from environmental conditions. The high ratings of certain violent programs indicate parental and societal approval, and imply family habits which exercise a much greater influence on children than does television drama. As one CBS television host observed later in 1972:

> [T]here are few monitoring parents who "turn off the TV like you turn off the vacuum cleaner when the rug is clean." Parents who let the TV run endlessly, "wind up with a spectator (child) who has no parent-child relationship, no peer group relationship."[26]

Clearly, those involved in writing, directing, producing, censoring, and broadcasting television shows believe that forces and factors outside their control dictate what the program fare shall be. If there are internal constraints and responsibilities affecting the substance of television programs, each of those groups tends to think these constraints and responsibilities lie with others. All groups, however, pay homage to the governing rule: the reality of the marketplace. As one producer said, the Nielsen ratings are "the only crap game in town."[27]

What this really means, as Professor Cantor pointed out, is that writers and producers mainly try to please the networks since "no program can ever be judged by the general audience unless it first pleases a buyer—in most cases, a network."[28] In sum, producers "would prefer to have the networks or parents take responsibility for the final effects of their programming efforts. The networks, because of their desire to sell products and please advertisers, seem to be concerned primarily with the size of the audience."[29] And because "Parents cannot be expected to have the sophistication to evaluate the short-term as well as long-term effects of programs on their children,"[30] there exists, in this critically important area, a large leadership vacuum.

7

REACHING A JUDGMENT

When the Surgeon General's Scientific Advisory Committee began to sift the research, it faced a formidable body of literature. Between August 1969 and April 1970, the staff had reviewed forty-six formal research proposals. Most had been solicited, but all were subjected to a "peer review" process which is traditional for the National Institutes of Health. This meant that an ad hoc committee was set up to evaluate the proposals and select the most meritorious ones. The review committee's composition changed for the different tasks, but always included were: members of the standing review committees of the NIMH; one or two members of the Surgeon General's Advisory Committee; and other social scientists considered to be experts in the particular field. One-half of the proposals survived this screening; twenty-three independent research projects were funded. They involved 7,500 youngsters ranging in age from three to nineteen and coming from all areas of the United States and all socioeconomic groups.[1] Additionally, a number of papers were commissioned, including reviews of the literature as well as analyses and critiques of both earlier and new research. In sum, there were sixty technical documents upon which the Surgeon General's Committee had to pass judgment and reach a conclusion.[2]

The final Report formally acknowledged that "the projects vary widely in subject, scope, and approach. . . ."[3] They also varied in quality. Douglas Fuchs, senior research coordinator during the period when the contracts were let, helped in selecting a number of them. But his caustic opinion, expressed later, was: "With few exceptions . . . the surveys are superficial, ungeneralizable exercises in opportunistic grantsmanship for the sake of political expediency."[4] Fuchs declared:

> The experiments on short-term TV effects are substantively spotty; the micro-analytical studies are entirely too expensive and micro-oriented for this project, the observational studies are conceptually very weak and will not likely be implemented properly, and the content analysis is as myopic as it is irrelevant to the whole project.[5]

These, it must be noted, are the views of a staff member who was keenly disappointed after his recommendation for a total research strategy had been rejected.

A majority of those directly involved in the research take a more balanced view. One experienced communications researcher who both conducted his own study and reviewed a large segment of all the research to prepare an overview paper, summed it up: "Some of the work was of high quality. Some of the studies were an embarrassment."[6] A member of the Advisory Committee remarked: "If you have twenty-three separate studies which then mushroom into forty-odd papers, I think it is inevitable that there is going to be high quality stuff, and stuff that is not of high quality."[7]

Everyone was aware of the limitations both of time and availability of senior researchers. A frequent sticking point was methodology. Committee member Ithiel de Sola Pool thought it natural there should be differences about whether the researchers' methodologies were sound. He pointed out that the methodological approach to the investigation of economic problems is so well established that economists are judged by their peers more on the basis of how they use the accepted tools than on the way they interpret the results. But behavioral scientists in the "softer" disciplines have sharp disagreements on methodology, thus compounding the disagreement over results.

Perhaps the most troublesome factor at work as the Advisory

Committee started sifting and sorting the research results was the atmosphere of suspicion. Six months after the appointment of the Advisory Committee, the fact that a veto had been exercised by the television industry became publicly known. This disclosure, through an article in *Science* magazine, on May 22, 1970, produced much indignation in the academic community.[8] Some of those vetoed were the senior explorers in the difficult terrain of television's effect on children. They included: Albert Bandura, of Stanford University, perhaps the most eminent of social scientists performing laboratory research on television and aggression; Leo Bogart, an official of the American Newspaper Publishers Association and author of a book on television; psychologist Leonard Berkowitz, of the University of Wisconsin, whose research findings indicated that aggressive films stimulated aggressive behavior in individuals of various ages; Leon Eisenberg, professor of child psychiatry at The Johns Hopkins Medical School, whose articles had included criticisms of the research done by the networks; Ralph Garry, a consultant to the Senate Juvenile Delinquency Committee in the early 1960s; Otto Larsen, professor of sociology at the University of Washington, who contributed to the Eisenhower Commission's volume, *Mass Media and Violence;* and Percy Tannenbaum, a psychologist teaching at the Graduate School of Public Policy at the University of California, Berkeley, whose writings and public testimony had been supportive of the hypothesis that violence viewing was related to subsequent aggressiveness.

Surgeon General Stewart had invited industry review of the list of nominees, he said in his original letter to the network presidents, "because the studies initiated by this group may involve the active collaboration of the television industry." Thus, he wished to "insure that all members of the advisory committee are acceptable to the major networks."[9] Stewart had evidently seen no reason to exclude two officials and three regular consultants of the networks from serving on his Committee. One critic, Matilda Paisley of Stanford, wrote later:

> If one accepts the premise that all major viewpoints should be represented so that no group can point an accusing finger after the committee has completed its work, then one would expect to see both Joseph Klapper [of CBS] and Albert Bandura on the committee. But if one argues that individuals publicly committed to one line of evidence would not be sufficiently

impartial to the new evidence, then one would expect to see neither Joseph Klapper nor Albert Bandura on the committee.[10]

The American Psychological Association and the American Anthropological Association registered strong protests upon learning of the industry veto. Anthony Wallace submitted his resignation as a Committee member. (Subsequently, he was persuaded to stay on.) In its final Report, the Committee unanimously labelled the veto process "a serious error."[11]

Although CBS had made a statesmanlike response in rejecting use of the tendered veto, Dr. Joseph Klapper, the CBS man on the Advisory Committee, proved to be an object of suspicion by some of the Committee staff and at least one of his fellow Committee members. He had written widely on the theme that whatever effects television might have, they occurred among a milieu of other influences. As recently as 1968, in testimony before the Eisenhower Violence Commission, Klapper had expressed doubts about any causal relationship between television violence and aggressive behavior in children. Rebutting Klapper, Alberta Siegel, who was to become a fellow member of the Surgeon General's Advisory Committee, had replied:

> To the media spokesmen, one is tempted to reply "Media man speaks with forked tongue." The television industry exists and reaps its profits from the conviction that television viewing does affect behavior—buying behavior.[12]

One cause of continuing suspicion about Klapper was his failure to apprise the Committee at its early meetings of what kinds of research CBS was conducting on its own. Not until the spring of 1970—after the staff had contracted most of its own research projects—did Dr. Klapper reveal details about research in progress at CBS.

It is a common occurrence in committee investigations for the staff responsible for developing basic evidence to become more zealous than the committee charged with evaluating that evidence. The Surgeon General's Advisory Committee on Television and Social Behavior was no exception. Senior research coordinator Douglas Fuchs became increasingly unhappy with the way the Committee was approaching its task and convinced that the whole operation was a political exercise rather than a scientific exploration. When he presented his research design at the September

1969 meeting, according to a colleague's observations, Fuchs felt the Committee had attacked him personally. He was particularly distressed because the Committee's criticisms of his research plan were unaccompanied by suggestions for alternative approaches. The Advisory Committee did not list priorities, did not establish guidelines for acceptable methodological designs, and did not encourage examination of any particular variables they thought could be important. The staff was left on its own.

Eli Rubinstein, vice-chairman of the Committee and senior staff member, was not unduly alarmed either by the Committee's industry representation, its general approach, or its acidulous reactions to staff proposals. An experienced bureaucrat and long-time observer of governmental advisory committees, he was reconciled to the fact that the staff would have to take the early initiatives while the Committee itself would have the final say. But Fuchs thought Rubinstein's conciliatory approach toward every issue meant that the effort would ultimately go nowhere. He left in June 1970, embittered after his one-year contract was not renewed.

Fuchs was not the only staff member who had doubts about whether the Committee would permit meaningful conclusions to be reached. His successor as senior research coordinator, George Comstock, later remarked that staff members habitually referred to the Committee as "the network five, the naive four, and the scientific three."[13] Some members of the Committee continued to see signs of an industry clique. Dr. Siegel commented afterward that she had never before served on a group with so many tensions and hostilities. Others thought her impressions were exaggerated. Dr. Pool recalled that when differences of opinion arose, rarely were the members of the alleged "industry five" aligned as one faction.

Paradoxically, the controversy produced by the revelation that the industry had been given a veto helped lead to a decision that was of major importance: the construction of a unanimous report. To the gratification of Dr. Rubinstein, members of the Committee agreed with him that the way to salvage the Committee's integrity was to reach common agreement on what the research really meant. (One of those emphatic about the need for unanimity was NBC's Dr. Coffin.) As the research reports started to come in during the summer of 1971, the Committee's work began in earnest.

Some of the new evidence, it was felt, was clear and important, either confirming earlier hypotheses or adding new dimensions to the whole subject. George Gerbner's analysis of current programs left no doubt that television fare was not, despite repeated industry pledges, becoming less violent. Almost all of the new laboratory experiments and the field studies tended to confirm the hypothesis that viewing televised violence produces heightened aggressiveness in some children, at least for the short run. The Stein–Friedrich study demonstrated the positive possibilities of television as a social learning tool by measuring prosocial effects of "Mister Rogers' Neighborhood."

What was impressive to the Advisory Committee was that when researchers measured relationships between dozens of variables in many settings by several methodologies, the presence of one variable (the child's viewing of violent television sequences) was associated most consistently with a second variable (the child's subsequent tendency to act more aggressively). The Committee members were not overly impressed with the statistical significance or the accounting for variance of any single study. They *were* impressed with the central finding of so many studies.

Inevitably, the effort at synthesizing the research findings produced misunderstandings. For example, the study by Dr. Monroe Lefkowitz and his colleagues in upstate New York was the first effort to measure the effects of televised violence over time. But the "cross-lagged analysis" by which they reached their conclusions was sharply questioned. The staff, and later the Committee, asked Dr. Lefkowitz and his colleagues to provide additional information and to rework some of the analyses. They asked other researchers to confirm this use of methodological tools. Finally, they took it upon themselves to reinterpret certain aspects of the Lefkowitz study. Concluding that the Committee was prejudiced against their work, Lefkowitz and his colleagues later publicly complained about the treatment.[14] Committee member Pool, on the other hand, felt they should be grateful for the Committee's effort to strengthen and clarify the meaning of their study. He wrote to Dr. Lefkowitz explaining that because Committee members had believed the study to be "of seminal importance," they had felt compelled by the data to make "some reinterpretations."[15] As he read Dr. Lefkowitz' complaint, Pool commented:

> I kept having a fantasy of Columbus waxing indignant at someone who maintained that the land he had discovered was not the Indies and feeling that his discovery was being derogated because others recognized the need to reinterpret what it was.[16]

Most of the new evidence contradicted Seymour Feshbach's earlier hypothesis that violence could have a cathartic effect. (Feshbach's new study for the Committee had already led him to revise that hypothesis and advance the possibility that televised fantasy provided a vicarious outlet for aggressive tendencies in some children even if realistic violence might encourage active aggressiveness.)[17] Meanwhile, Dr. Gerbner had decided that action violence was not nearly so important as symbolic violence (portrayals and dramatizations of individuals, groups of people, and values which caused children to develop unreal and unhealthy attitudes towards various aspects of the world around them).[18]

The most certain conclusion the Committee could logically reach was that the aggregate research effort demonstrated how many questions were left unanswered. Such a conclusion would not suffice, however. Senator Pastore had expressed the fervent hope that the Committee's findings would not be couched in "a lot of ifs and buts" but would permit the Surgeon General to "tell us in very simple language whether or not the broadcasters ought to be put on notice."[19] What the Committee had to do, as it acknowledged, was "to come to as carefully objective a conclusion as the data warranted."[20]

By the early fall of 1971, the writing of the Report got underway. To report on the research, the Committee divided itself into three subcommittees, each responsible for a group of studies: Patterns of Use; Television and Social Learning; and Television and Adolescent Aggressiveness. Here, too, misunderstandings arose. When the subcommittee responsible for Television and Adolescent Aggressiveness had its first meeting to review a draft chapter summing up the research under this heading—a draft prepared by senior research coordinator George Comstock—only two of the five-member subcommittee were present: Ira Cisin of George Washington University and Joseph Klapper, research director of CBS. Armed with pages of specific suggestions, Klapper insisted that it be redrafted. Several more drafts were attempted before one shaped by Ithiel Pool was finally accepted by the subcommittee.

Staff members continued to see evidence of an industry-inspired faction. Others, more benevolent, thought the problem was more related to available time. Members with teaching responsibilities had less time to give to the entire effort, including the writing of the Report, than did those whose livelihoods came from industry research in this field. The academicians were thus less involved in suggesting contextual "qualifications" and honing careful phrases. Quite aside from motives, the function of available time and energy clearly affected the language and tone of the Report.

The variety of the studies made it hard to put the pieces together. There was usually more than one way to interpret the data. Dr. Klapper was one who thought the differences of opinion about the way to interpret the research results mainly stemmed from differences in professional backgrounds.

> There were twelve people there representing several different disciplines and, as is always the case in these situations, some of them had a point of view on the matter and some of them didn't, and the points of view differed. . . . I found it to be an exceptionally smooth running Committee. I saw no factions. . . . I never saw any major fight. . . . I would say that the differences that existed were differences in emphasis in research orientation. That is, there is a hell of a long way between an Irving Janis, who is an experimentalist and a goddam good one, and a Charles Pinderhughes, who is a psychoanalyst and a goddam good one. . . . So naturally there were differences in the degree of weight which different individuals would give to any individual piece of evidence.[21]

Dr. Klapper perceived the major differences to be between Committee and staff:

> I saw no glaring across the table. I saw considerable problems between the Committee on the one side and staff on the other. And I think that's par for the course, unfortunately. I think that this is one of the most unfortunate aspects of these kinds of enterprises; I think it is absolutely inevitable that there will be serious friction between commission and staff, always.[22]

Then there was the problem, as Robert Liebert noted, that "almost all experimental studies have some methodological flaws."[23] In the case of the new studies, however, Dr. Liebert's "overview" emphasized that "each of these flaws tends to be unique rather than shared by all of the investigators."[24] Finally, even if the design, the research itself, and the interpretation of the results were all sound, there remained "no easy answer to the question of their external applicability."[25]

Thus did many factors—quality, interpretation, and relationship of research findings; professional perspective and occupational affiliation; suspicions about motives; antagonisms between Committee and staff; available time and energies—all contribute to the Report for the United States Surgeon General entitled *Television and Growing Up: The Impact of Televised Violence.* Never believing in the possibility that a single "critical experiment" would produce a single irrefutable answer, the Committee reached its conclusions on the basis of the accumulated weight of evidence.

Eli Rubinstein made a final suggestion which helped pave the way for a unanimous Report. It was that the personal conclusions of the Committee members not included in their common research assessments might be collected into a wrap-up chapter, "The Unfinished Agenda," which would not bear the Committee's official stamp. That being agreed upon, Rubinstein's 1971 Thanksgiving was a very special one. By that date he had successfully shepherded the members of the Surgeon General's Advisory Committee onto a single platform.

The long-awaited Report, formally transmitted to the Surgeon General, consisted of 137 pages divided into nine chapters, plus another thirty pages of appendices. (Adding the five volumes of research reports with "overviews," he was handed almost 2,500 pages to digest.) Scientific caution and the quest for consensus provided understandable restraints in the drafting process. Less understandable was the evidence of a final haste in putting the Report into print that resulted in a poorly written document with few of the encapsulating sentences or paragraphs that would provide clarity for the layman. The reader could search in vain for the kind of thoughtful summation which the prolonged deliberations should have produced.

But restraint accomplished the unanimity which had been the goal of the Committee. All twelve members signed the transmittal letter to the Surgeon General on January 19, 1972. All twelve endorsed the conclusion, masterful in its caution:

> Thus, the two sets of findings [experimental and survey] converge in three respects: a preliminary and tentative indication of a causal relation

between viewing violence on television and aggressive behavior; an indication that any such causal relation operates only on some children (who are predisposed to be aggressive); and an indication that it operates only in some environmental contexts. Such tentative and limited conclusions are not very satisfying. They represent substantially more knowledge than we had two years ago, but they leave many questions unanswered.[26]

The Committee knew the Report would not be received uncritically. So did Surgeon General Jesse Steinfeld, the successor to Dr. Stewart, who received the Report and made it public. Dr. Steinfeld declared:

This report will undoubtedly be scrutinized carefully by people who will be looking for support for their own point of view. Individuals with strong convictions on either side of the question about the effects of televised violence may not be satisfied. What these individuals will fail to recognize is that this set of conclusions, for the first time in this field of inquiry, sets a solid and extensive base of evidence in an appropriate perspective. In that sense, the report and the research on which it is based represent a major contribution.[27]

THE REPORT GOES PUBLIC

Shortly after launching the Advisory Committee on Television and Social Behavior, Surgeon General Stewart resigned to take a university post. His successor, like Stewart, was a medical doctor and a career Public Health Service Officer. Also like Stewart, Dr. Jesse Steinfeld found that the title he assumed sounded more important than the job really was.

In earlier days, the Surgeon General of the United States Public Health Service enjoyed considerable status as the chief civilian health officer of the federal government. Until the mid-1960s, he was directly responsible for overseeing almost all the government's major health programs—from hospital construction, to biomedical research, to supervision of the Public Health Service Commissioned Corps and more than one hundred PHS hospitals. With the passage of Medicare and Medicaid in 1965, and the new health manpower support programs in 1966, the federal government's health responsibilities grew dramatically and so did its health bureaucracy. So that new functions might be better performed, reorganization occurred throughout the bureaucracy.

NIMH had traditionally been under the Public Health Service; it remained so while becoming part of HEW's Health Services and Mental Health Administration in the reorganization of 1967.

77

Though the NIMH budget and activities flourished, the old functions of the Public Health Service declined in relative importance. So did the status of the Surgeon General. In 1966, the position of Assistant Secretary of HEW for Health and Scientific Affairs was created. With that move, the chief civilian health officer of the federal government became a political appointee. (Surgeon Generals, though often selected for political reasons, had traditionally come from the corps of career health officers.)

Dr. Steinfeld knew when he moved into the Surgeon General's office that it had lost most of its organizational base and much of its prestige. Despite the rank and title, he was now a staff officer reporting to the Assistant Secretary. His role was not necessarily unimportant, particularly if there was a close relationship between the Surgeon General and the Assistant Secretary. Surgeon General Steinfeld did have a close relationship with Dr. Roger Egeberg, the Assistant Secretary for Health and Scientific Affairs. However, Egeberg remained in that position for less than a year, and with his departure, the Surgeon General lost much of his remaining influence.

Senator Pastore's call for the television inquiry, directed specifically to the Surgeon General, gave a boost to the office. Yet Dr. Steinfeld must have considered this a mixed blessing at best. His first task in connection with the Surgeon General's Advisory Committee was to try to explain to Pastore and the public why his predecessor had allowed the television networks the privilege of vetoing nominees for the Committee.[1] The task was made especially difficult, because on his explanation partially rested the worth, and indeed the effective continuance, of the Advisory Committee. Furthermore, Steinfeld personally believed that his predecessor's reliance on the Smoking Committee precedent was a serious error.

In September 1971, before the Advisory Committee had synthesized the completed research into a report, several of the researchers presented papers on their own findings at the annual meeting of the American Psychological Association. This was done with the cognizance of the Surgeon General's office and with the specific blessing of Dr. Rubinstein. Senator Pastore's staff also had been forewarned. But press coverage of the papers by Professors Liebert, Lyle, Greenberg, and Chaffee produced more publicity than anyone had foreseen. Pastore called Dr. Steinfeld before his committee to ask whether the members of the American Psychological Association were getting the answers before those who had commissioned the study.[2] Actually, said Pastore, he knew that that wasn't quite the case; he understood that some of the researchers had merely presented "working papers."[3]

> But frankly if you had not been a member of this committee and you were just a private citizen who was interested in what progress had been made, you would have gotten the wrong impression. . . . I thought one of the chief reasons of bringing you here today is so that we could get this straightened out as to exactly what the situation is, whether or not these panel discussions were the opinion of your Advisory Committee, and naturally, of course, when a final report would be forthcoming.
>
> I think that the public is entitled to know at this juncture just about where we stand, and when we can have something definitive so that action can be taken.[4]

Dutifully and carefully, the Surgeon General explained:

> It has been our policy, in keeping with the principle of scientific freedom, to permit the researchers participating in our program to publish independently or to discuss their findings at appropriate scientific meetings.
>
> This recent symposium is the first time a group of participating researchers have presented their completed work at a scientific meeting. . . . I should emphasize that these individual investigators are not speaking for the Scientific Advisory Committee, whose responsibility it is to examine carefully all the evidence now accumulated and report to me its findings and conclusions.[5]

On December 31, 1971, the long-awaited Report was informally transmitted to the Surgeon General. Before it was officially released or before Dr. Steinfeld could begin to digest its meaning, *The New York Times* published a page-one story giving its own interpretation of what the Scientific Advisory Committee had found.

On January 11, the *Times'* scoop appeared. The cautious language of the Committee was summed up by long-time television critic Jack Gould in a lead paragraph:

> The office of the United States Surgeon General has found that violence in television programming does not have an adverse effect on the majority of the nation's youth but may influence small groups of youngsters predisposed by many factors to aggressive behavior.[6]

Gould's summary contained one serious specific error. Despite the qualifications that the Committee put on its findings, nowhere did it say that only "small groups" of children were affected. Indeed, the Committee specified that the children so influenced might constitute either "a small portion or a substantial portion of the total population of young television viewers." But then to compound this error beyond all meaning, the front-page headline in the *Times* ran: "TV Violence Held Unharmful to Youth."[7]

Dr. Steinfeld soon realized that any control he might be able to exercise over the Report's publicity had been grossly undermined by this premature, erroneous, and mysterious disclosure in the *Times*. Controversy was not long in coming. Representative John M. Murphy of New York, who had been watching the Committee with suspicion since he had learned of the industry "veto," charged that the Committee, "heavily loaded in favor of the industry," had produced a report that was nothing but a whitewash.[8] Then the *Times* further complicated matters. Warning in an editorial against the dangers of televised violence whatever the precise scientific evidence, the *Times* on January 15 repeated Gould's faulty summation that "the majority of young people are not adversely affected," but only those "small groups" already "predisposed to aggressive behavior."[9]

Some Committee members darkly suspected that selected portions of the study had been made available to Gould via a New York television industry connection. Their suspicion was fueled by the prompt wide-scale distribution of the *Times'* story by the National Association of Broadcasters to its members and friends.*

On January 17, the Surgeon General tried to clarify public understanding of what his Committee had found. At a news conference in Washington, Dr. Steinfeld placed emphasis where he thought it ought to be: "[T]he study shows for the first time a causal connection between violence shown on television and subsequent [aggressive] behavior by children."[10] He added emphatically: "This study is not a whitewash." While conceding that some of the evidence was "inconclusive and not very satisfying,"

---

*Gould has since stated that he had no problem obtaining a leaked text of the summary report. Without revealing his source, he commented wryly: ". . . the headache came in turning down more copies of the document. I wound up with four copies." (Letter from Jack Gould to Stephen Strickland, Spring 1974).

the Surgeon General thought the Report provided "a basis for intelligent action by the networks, the FCC and the Congress."[11]

But the Committee's heavily qualified conclusions and often abstruse language resulted in widely varying press accounts. Michael Putney, writing in *The National Observer*, presented a lively treatment.

> Beep, beep!
> Move over Road Runner, 'cause here come a dozen distinguished behavioral scientists who say that watching your antics and other violence-laden TV fare may be hazardous to some kids' mental health.
> Television violence, the scientists emphasize, does not have a "uniformly adverse effect on the majority of children," but kids who are already violence prone may be spurred on to yet more aggressive anti-social behavior after watching it on the tube.[12]

The story's caption was: "TV Gets a Slap, Not a Wallop, For Violence."

Norman Mark, television editor of the *Chicago Daily News*, wrote two articles on the Report, which were carried in a number of newspapers across the country. His lead sentence reached an opposite conclusion from that of Gould and Putney:

> Dynamite is hidden in the surgeon general's report on children and television violence, for the report reveals that most children are definitely and adversely affected by televised mayhem.[13]

The *Birmingham News* had a special front-page banner to call attention to Mark's story: "Scientists say TV violence DOES influence children." But the [Washington] *Evening Star* headlined its report on the Surgeon General's press conference: "TV Violence Study Called Whitewash," and began its story:

> A government-funded study cautiously concludes that televised crime and violence contribute in only a small way to violence in America.[14]

Broadcasting magazine headlined its report: "Violence on Air and in Life: No Clear Link"; and its subhead summarized: "Million-dollar study, at last complete, identified stronger influences [than TV] behind hostile acts of the young." The story's lead paragraph:

> A blue-ribbon committee of social scientists has concluded that there is no causal relationship between television programs that depict violence and aggressive behavior by the majority of children.[15]

Dr. Steinfeld had correctly predicted that persons of strong fixed persuasions about televised violence would not be satisfied with the Report. Amid the conflicting press accounts, even those whose minds were open to persuasion had difficulty understanding what the Report really said. Some strongly concerned citizens already believed that programs watched by children should be stripped of all violence and that the scientific debates about precise effects of violence were a waste of time. William Abbott, president of the Foundation to Improve Television, declared: "The studies still continue, all the while our children are still—this afternoon, tomorrow, and next week—being force-fed the steady diet of violence."[16] His organization pressed forward with law suits seeking injunctions against the showing of particularly violent programs.

A number of social scientists were equally outraged. Those who had worked in the field of television and social learning were confused. Some who had done research for the Committee thought the Report had misinterpreted their findings. A few were moved to adopt a new posture, becoming advocates rather than researchers. Professor Robert Liebert provides a case in point. Because of his earlier work in the field, the staff of the Advisory Committee approached him in 1969 to submit a proposal for new research that would further clarify aggressive effects of television. He did so. In addition, he was asked to review related research and develop an overview paper of five major research projects relating to "Television and Social Learning." Professor Liebert had summarized the evidence as follows:

> At least under some circumstances, exposure to televised aggression can lead children to accept what they have seen as a partial guide for their own actions. As a result, the present entertainment offerings of the television medium may be contributing, in some measure, to the aggressive behavior of many normal children. Such an effect has now been shown in a wide variety of situations.[17]

Dr. Liebert provided a further summation at the September meeting of the American Psychological Association and also discussed his and the other research findings in his classes at Stony Brook. When the *Times'* story appeared, his students questioned him sharply, and Liebert decided that he had an additional obligation as a social scientist. His and his colleagues' work, he believed, was being misinterpreted.[18] Resorting to public forums, Liebert sought to redress what he believed was an injustice and to prevent the inaction that he feared the misinterpretations would lead to. As a social scientist, Liebert continued to follow his training and "to avoid statements of certainty." But as he told *The New York Times,* the studies, added to earlier research, "quite clearly" demonstrate "that watching violence in a television context can instigate aggressive behavior in children."[19] As for what he proposed be done, the *Times* quoted Liebert:

> We don't want to take the babysitter away, we just want to stop her from committing murder in the living room.[20]

Subsequently in his testimony before the Pastore committee, Liebert had a two-step proposal for reform:

> [O]ne, an immediate and sharp decrease in the amount of violence in programs directed primarily to children; and, two, an equally enthusiastic effort to increase the number of programs designed to teach positive lessons.[21]

Carl Perian, who had been the staff director of the Dodd Committee when it investigated this issue in 1964, had since joined the staff of Congressman John M. Murphy of New York. Now he encouraged Murphy in his effort to "get at the truth" about the new evidence, declaring: "It isn't a question of opinion or even judgment, it's a matter of looking at the documents, and concluding that, yes, indeed, the Surgeon General's report is misleading."[22] Perian argued that neither he nor the congressman had any doubt "that the report is a fraud—purposeful fraud."[23]

Albert Bandura had maintained a dignified silence throughout the period of the Advisory Committee's existence. He had made no complaint about being vetoed or about the implicit questioning of the "objectivity" of his research. Now, encouraged by Congressman Murphy to give his views, Bandura lashed out at the Scientific Advisory Committee:

> The Surgeon General's Report demonstrates that the television industry is sufficiently powerful to control how research bearing on the psychological effects of televised violence is officially evaluated and reported to the general public. . . . The irate researchers whose findings were irresponsibly distorted in the Surgeon General's Report are fully justified in the objections they have raised. . . . [A] double standard is used in evaluating individual studies

depending on how their findings relate to the industry viewpoint. . . . The report concludes on a high moral tone. . . . It is unfortunate that these moral concerns did not operate more forcefully within the advisory committee itself. . . . This sorry case further illustrates the need for procedures to ensure that in the future scientific advisory panels will not be controlled by the very industries whose practices they are supposed to evaluate.[24]

Dr. Jack Lyle, like Liebert both a researcher and an "overviewer" for the Committee, offered one suggestion to his fellow social scientists who wondered, amid all the confusion, what the new research really showed. Addressing the International Congress of Psychologists, he proposed that the official Report of the Advisory Committee *not* be relied upon as a summary of the research evidence. Instead, he suggested, interested professionals should read the overview chapters in each of the five volumes of technical reports which provide a good summary of the research done.[25]

It was hardly a helpful suggestion to ordinary citizens or politicians who could not be expected to wade through such a mass of social science research literature. To assist the latter, Senator Pastore let it be known that he considered the Report a "major breakthrough" and scheduled hearings in late March 1972 to invite testimony about future policy implications. His plan was to ask the Surgeon General and his Advisory Committee members, network leaders, critics, and other interested parties "what steps each can and should take in the light of the Report's findings and conclusions." Putting a bright face on a troubled situation, the Rhode Island senator declared in advance:

> Now I want to know where do we go from here with what we've found out. I want recommendations. . . . I want to boil the Report down into one crystallized interpretation. That's what the hearings are going to do.[26]

9

NEW HEARINGS, NEW CONSENSUS?

> To everyone who has read it—laymen as well as scientists—it is apparent
> the report is couched in conservative, cautious terms. After all this is a highly
> complex subject. Nevertheless certain basic conclusions have emerged. Dur-
> ing the course of these hearings the committee will hear from the Surgeon
> General, members of his committee, and many of the experts who did origi-
> nal research for the report. Among other things, I would hope these distin-
> guished men and women will spell out as simply as possible for the benefit
> of us all what these conclusions are; and what steps the Surgeon General, the
> scientific community, the agencies of Government, and the broadcast indus-
> try can and should take in view of them.[1]

With those words, Senator Pastore opened the hearings of the
Senate Subcommittee on Communications on March 21, 1972—
three years to the month since he had spurred this search for a
scientific answer to a vexing social problem.

A small contretemps marked the beginning of the hearings.
Despite Pastore's insistence that the Surgeon General was "the
chief health officer of the United States of America," Dr. Merlin K.
DuVal, Assistant Secretary of HEW for Health and Scientific
Affairs, appeared with the intention of speaking for HEW on the
Report's meaning. Pastore and his Communications Counsel,
Nicholas Zapple, thought this would merely confuse matters. The
senator insisted that Dr. Steinfeld be the lead witness.

Pastore may have suspected that HEW was seeking to soft-pedal the Report's implications. In fact, the statement Dr. DuVal was prepared to make before the Committee was strong:

> I have reached some very definite conclusions, after a review of the Committee's report, and in consultation with my advisors on this subject . . . the most significant being that it is beyond dispute that a reduction in the violent content of television programming is most desirable.[2]

DuVal never got to testify, but later his remarks were entered in the printed record.

Steinfeld's testimony was equally unequivocal. Senator Pastore had asked earlier whether, based on the best scientific evidence, "broadcasters ought to be put on notice. . . ." Dr. Steinfeld now responded to that question:

> After review of the committee's report and the five volumes of original research undertaken at your request, as well as a review of the previous literature on the subject, my professional response today is that the broadcasters should be put on notice.[3]

Senator Pastore had expressed the hope that the Surgeon General, among others, would "spell out as simply as possible" what the Report's conclusions were. Dr. Steinfeld responded:

> While the committee report is carefully phrased and qualified in language acceptable to social scientists, it is clear to me that the causal relationship between televised violence and antisocial behavior is sufficient to warrant appropriate and immediate remedial action.[4]

The chairman wanted to be absolutely certain that there was no question in anyone's mind about the Surgeon General's position.

Pastore: You, Dr. Steinfeld, as the chief health officer of the United States of America, have said: ". . . there comes a time when the data are sufficient to justify action. That time has come."

Is that your unequivocal opinion?

Steinfeld: Yes, sir.

Pastore: And you reached that opinion from this report?

Steinfeld: From this report, the five volumes [of research findings], and other reading and attendance at a number of meetings.[5]

As the hearings continued, the chairman doggedly pressed each witness on this conclusion and its logical implications. He found an able testifier in Ithiel de Sola Pool, a distinguished political scientist, who, as a member of the Advisory Committee, had contributed importantly to developing conclusions on which all the Committee members could agree. Dr. Pool summed up the significance of the Report in one sentence:

> Twelve scientists of widely different views unanimously agreed that scientific evidence indicates that the viewing of television violence by young people causes them to behave more aggressively.[6]

News accounts which emphasized the qualifications to that scientific finding, said Pool, had "turned the report on its head." There had been good reasons for the Advisory Committee's caution in writing the Report. Pool explained:

> The qualifications are important and the report did the right thing in stressing them. We who work as scientists are all too often dismayed at the way a small partial finding gets blown up and distorted in popular reporting. Someone finds that a drug reduces the incidence of some cancers in rats and popular magazines announce a cancer cure. We could have written a careless report and said without further qualification that "violence on TV leads to violence in our society." The next day people would have been misusing the report to justify censorship and to frighten parents.[7]

Professor Ira Cisin added another explanation:

> This report has been referred to several times as a compromise report. In a sense it would have been a compromise if we had been writing about our opinions. To the extent that we tried to summarize and integrate a body of data, it was not a compromise, it was something we all agreed to.[8]

The testimony of the seven Advisory Committee members at Pastore's hearings was a replay of the different emphases and interests which each had brought to the Committee's deliberations. Dr. Pinderhughes reflected the sensitivities of a black psychiatrist who personally understood and had clinically observed adverse behavioral effects of racism, including that purveyed via television. He had, he declared, his own special "paranoia" about the meaning of televised violence.[9] Dr. Harold Mendelsohn thought more attention should be focused on the quantity of television violence content which produced adverse effects.[10] Dr. Cisin wanted to know more about the numbers of children affected.[11] It was Dr. Alberta Siegel's "guess" that "TV violence has negative effects on all child viewers, but that countervailing forces overcome these effects in the majority."[12] Dr. Klapper stressed the role of forces other than television as influences and the responsibility of parents.[13]

Despite the variations of emphasis, all the members of the Advisory Committee who were present agreed to the signal finding that, in Dr. Klapper's words, "there are certainly indications of a causal relationship" between televised violence and aggression by children.[14]

Senator Pastore took pains not to let other messages confuse this focus on the central conclusion. Addressing Dr. Klapper, the chairman said:

> You talk about the responsibility of the parents, and I agree with you.
> You talk about the maximization of professional programs. I agree with you.
> But, why don't we talk about the minimizing of excessive violence? Why isn't that part of the question? . . .
> You are a scientist with the broadcasting industry, CBS. It is one of the three networks. Don't you think there has been much violence on television that is unnecessary?
>
> Dr. Klapper: Yes.[15]

That agreed to, the chairman pressed Dr. Klapper about "why." Pastore was concerned, he said, about the suggestion that one reason the networks employed violence as a prominent feature of entertainment programming was that, being popular, violence produced profits. "If it is being done to get more advertising and more viewers, I say it is all wrong, and that is what we are talking about." Dr. Klapper replied: "I am not one to disagree with that statement, sir."[16]

Pastore asked NBC's Dr. Coffin a similar question: "Do you agree with this idea that there should be some action taken?" Dr. Coffin responded: "I think that, yes, I would agree with that."[17]

Those social scientists who came prepared to criticize the Report for over-cautious conclusions soon found themselves overtaken by events. When the aggrieved Dr. Lefkowitz appeared before the Committee to present his critique, he admitted that "the Surgeon General's Committee seems to have reversed its published position. . . ."[18] When Professor Leonard Berkowitz, one of the blackballed seven, sought to challenge the Advisory Committee's interpretations, Pastore interrupted him: "I don't think you were here yesterday, were you?"[19] Upon hearing what those he came to criticize had said, Dr. Berkowitz concluded that "a new consensus seems to be evolving at perhaps a stronger level than had initially existed. . . ."[20]

The hearings were a tribute to a purposeful chairman. Senator Pastore sought and drove home a clearly stated consensus: that the scientific study he had inspired and awaited so long showed, in the opinion of leading experts, a causal connection between televised violence and aggressive behavior—and something ought to be done about it. There remained the question about what to do—a question fraught with political and constitutional hazards. The carefully elicited scientific consensus had brought the policymakers only to the edge of decision.

Senator Pastore himself appeared uncertain of the next steps. He was obviously pleased at having saved the Report from the cross fire of its critics. In his judgment, there was no question that the networks ought to set about removing from the TV screens "gratuitous violence, unnecessary violence, violence for the sake of violence." Further, there ought to be more and better constructive programs. Pastore would have liked the network officials to pledge that they would take action on both fronts but stressed that although his concern was deep and longlived and his Committee's interest keen, "No one is going to begin to twist your arm. . . ." The senator was well aware that, "fundamentally, let's face it, this committee, this Congress, no one can censor programming."[21]

Members of the Senate Communications Subcommittee realized the need to help define courses of appropriate action, even if they might not be able to impose them. They wanted the help of the social scientists in arriving at those definitions. Senator Marlowe Cook voiced unhappiness with Dr. Steinfeld's caveat that the Advisory Committee had reported scientific findings but was constrained from making policy recommendations. He asked:

> If, in fact, the government is going to select a committee and if, in fact, we are going to spend $2 million of the people's money of this country and not come up with recommendations, even if they are recommendations that we sit down with the networks and try to work out a system, are we really doing our job?[22]

Senator Cook felt the position of the Surgeon General and his Advisory Committee was to "throw [the Report] in front of the

committee and say, now you asked for it, you do as you please."[23]
But Senator Howard Baker, the ranking minority member, was
more understanding of the Surgeon General's reluctance to do
other than offer broad guidelines.

> I agree with you, Doctor, that it is primarily the function of this subcom-
> mittee to translate your scientific advice and observations into legislative
> language, if any. And it is the function of the administrative agencies, in this
> case, the Federal Communications Commission, to hear and understand the
> best scientific opinion and translate it into policy.[24]

It was not that the scientific "experts" did not have thoughts
about appropriate actions. But, as Dr. Pool sought to explain,
"Too often scientists pontificate on public policy as if their science
has given them answers when their answers come from their personal values."[25] Dr. Pool told the Senate Subcommittee: "As to
what needs to be done, I would rather say as a citizen than a
scientist, because that is a civic question, not a scientific question."[26]

Clearly, the social scientists were unwilling to propose direct
government action to secure a reduction in televised violence.
Although Dr. Liebert had been most vociferous in calling for such
a reduction, he joined the others in shrinking from the suggestion
of censorship or control. As he later explained:

> [C]ensorship is a matter of great concern. The very kind of social-
> political orientation that makes people concerned about television violence
> goes hand-in-hand with concern against inviting more government control
> —entertainment today, news tomorrow.[27]

No one had been more outspoken than Dr. Alberta Siegel in criticizing network officials for failure to heed social scientists' warnings and parents' concerns, but even she would not recommend
specific government restraints. Instead, Dr. Siegel offered a list of
five concrete suggestions for private and public follow-up action.
As she testified to the Committee:

> I have several suggestions of alternatives to self-regulation. The first one
> I want to make is. . . . We need an independent monitoring agency to provide
> regular reports on the level of violence in television entertainment. . . . I think
> these reports should be broadcast over television and should appear in
> newspapers and magazines, these smog reports on violence pollution. They
> should indicate how much violence is occurring, which networks and stations

are broadcasting it, the times it is being broadcast, and how many child viewers are estimated to be watching at those times. . . .

Second, I suggest that consumers convey their disapproval of violence vendors in two ways. We may refuse to purchase their products. And we may refuse to buy stock in their firms. . . .

A third suggestion derives from my observation that TV producers are mimics. . . . When successful new formats of non-violent entertainment are devised, they will be copied. I recommend increased support for public television because I believe that the craftsmen in public television are likely to turn their energies and talents to creating constructive programs for children. . . .

It is the imitative capabilities of TV producers that prompt my fourth suggestion as well. . . . I recommend that travel fellowships be offered to the writers and producers of children's television programs so that they may observe firsthand how our neighboring nations . . . have succeeded in attracting child audiences without saturating them with violence.

Fifth, I believe the Federal Communications Commission could be more effective in obtaining fair treatment for children and adolescents. I suggest that a child advocate be appointed to the staff of the FCC. This individual should have frequent and direct communications with the Commissioners, advising them on questions bearing on the welfare of children. He or she should be well acquainted with social scientific research and also in close communication with the professions serving children. . . .[28]

Government officials also suggested courses of action they were prepared to take. Dr. Steinfeld reported that consultations were already underway involving his office, NIMH, the Office of Child Development in HEW, and the FCC. In addition, the Office of Child Development was preparing a booklet for parents on the potential benefits and dangers of television for children and how to utilize the medium appropriately.[29]

FCC Chairman Dean Burch, registering strong concern over the Advisory Committee's findings, firmly stated his belief "that the response of the broadcasting industry to the Surgeon General's report should be immediate and decisive—and that it should proceed along two parallel but distinct tracks: First, the reduction to near-zero of all gratuitous and needless violence in the programming that is specifically directed to children or that children tend to watch in large numbers; and second, the creation of substantial amounts of new and diversified programming, not just the usual diet of cartoons, designed to open the eyes and expand the minds of young viewers."[30] Burch proposed that the FCC hold public panel discussions on all aspects of children's television, and continuing informal discussions with network officials. Beyond that, he said, "I cannot come before you today with the answers, either tentative or definitive, as to the governmental actions that might be called for."[31]

A minor storm was provoked by FCC member Nicholas Johnson who had long played the role of gadfly to the broadcast industry. In an emotionally charged testimony, Johnson now accused the network heads of being "a vicious, evil influence"[32] who had "molested the minds of our Nation's children to serve the cause of corporate profit."[33] He added:

> If you do it [molest a child] during the week, on the school playground, to one child, you are driven off to prison in a police car. But if you do it on Saturday morning, in the living room, to millions of young children, you are just driven home, by a chauffeur, in a long, black limousine.[34]

He proposed a massive subsidy of $500 million for public broadcasting and further urged: 1) the three commercial networks provide one-third of all prime time on a nonsponsored, staggered basis for entertainment, dramatic, cultural, and public affairs programming; 2) counteradvertising should be required; 3) two commercial minutes should be removed from every half-hour containing violence and given to responsible professionals who would convey balancing information; 4) tort actions should be brought against the networks by victims of violent actions; 5) the present number of commercial minutes should be cut by one-half; 6) all commercials should be grouped at the end of a program; 7) the networks should be prohibited from owning programs, program production facilities, or stations; and 8) funding should be provided for the continuing review of the impact of television on all aspects of our society.[35]

Johnson's outburst stirred immediate resentment. To Pastore's inquiry, Chairman Burch replied, "[W]e get this kind of performance almost every day at the Commission, and very candidly we are not impressed by a lot of the conclusions that Commissioner Johnson draws. I think that the bulk of his recommendations are actually irrelevant, it seems to me, to the question of television violence."[36] Senator Baker was even more critical. Sharply rebuking Johnson, Baker said:

I feel an outrage, Mr. Johnson, that you have brought to this hearing a trauma of emotionalism that will positively impede our progress in trying to arrive at a sensible solution to a real problem. . . .[37]

One quite specific proposal to emerge had earlier been put forward at a conference sponsored by the Aspen Program on Communications and Society by Lloyd M. Morrisett, president of the Markle Foundation, and Orville G. Brim, Jr., former president of Russell Sage Foundation. In Morrisett's words:

We are impressed by the need for techniques to monitor on a continuing basis the amount and quality of violence on television as a means of informing the public and allowing a more complete understanding of the problem. In suggesting an attack on this problem, we fully understand the complexity of the issue. It will be difficult to design sound measures of violence on television and the first ones will undoubtedly be imperfect and need to be improved over time. Despite this and other problems we believe the issue is important enough to warrant immediate action.[38]

The idea appealed to Senator Pastore. On the final day of the hearings, he read a statement to the assembled government and broadcast witnesses calling on HEW Secretary Elliot Richardson to have his department, in consultation with the FCC, take a lead in developing "a measurement for violence on television so that a report can be submitted annually to this Committee on the level of violence entering American homes."[39]

Many of the witnesses at the hearings voiced approval of this endeavor. However, Senator Baker had reservations. Would a violence index, he asked, tend to have the reverse effect of the Nielsen ratings? Would competing networks be satisfied simply to gain slightly lower violence ratings for their programs?

But the Secretary of HEW, Elliot Richardson, sent word:

Staff of the NIMH are presently actively involved in discussing with experts in the field both theoretical and methodological issues in developing indices of the meaning and effects of TV programming. . . . By June 30 we will be able to provide you with our best judgment on the feasibility of developing such an index.[40]

Chairman Burch of the FCC pledged to cooperate. But he entered a cautionary note in a letter to Senator Pastore: "The cooperation of all the industries involved will be crucial to our success."[41]

The hearings adjourned in a spirit of high concern if somewhat vague purpose. There were cynics watching. Dr. Albert Bandura had earlier predicted that whatever response the Pastore hearings might engender at the time, from the television industry and the government, all would soon evaporate. Asked what were the prospects for remedial action, Bandura replied: "My general impression is that congressional hearings are sort of like television reruns: same characters, same plot, same outcome."[42]

10

THE ONSLAUGHT OF THE CRITICS

Committee and staff members were well aware that the Surgeon General's Report would be carefully scrutinized, but, beyond cautious phrasing, there was little they could do to control how the Report would be interpreted by both professionals and the press. According to Dr. Rubinstein, "one of the reasons the message sent is often not the message received, is the proclivity of the press to emphasize the sensational and ignore the substance."[1] Press coverage during the entire course of the Surgeon General's Committee deliberations was surprisingly inadequate. By far the greatest coverage before the Report was released dealt with controversy over the industry's blackballing of certain nominees for the Committee. Then *The New York Times'* scoop—a week before the Report's release—got press treatment off to a totally misleading start.

When the Report was finally issued, most of the immediate publicity dealt only sketchily with its findings and placed more emphasis on its style as well as the motives and machinations of the participants. Some of the analyses accepted uncritically the first erroneous account of *The New York Times* or the Washington *Evening Star.* Others recognized that the Report concluded more than that, but found it too difficult to wade through the abstruse prose. *Newsweek's* Joseph Morgenstern, in an article on filmmaking entitled "The New Violence," was highly critical of the Report's language:

> Whether by intent or ineptitude, the committee misrepresented some of the data, ignored some of it, and buried all of it alive in prose that was obviously meant to be unreadable and unread.[2]

But Morgenstern did mention *The New York Times'* error, pointing out that according to the Report the violence-prone viewers might constitute a small or substantial portion of young persons.

A number of critics attacked the Report for its inconclusiveness. Norman Mark, television editor of the *Chicago Daily News*, concluded that the fuzziness of the Report resulted from the Committee's desire "to satisfy all sides of the issue."[3] In the spring 1972 issue of *Journal of Broadcasting*, Professor James Anderson of Ohio University issued a harsh verdict: That portion of the Report laying out the potential role—good and bad—that television can play was "an incredibly unsophisticated discussion"; some of the research studies contained "fanciful interpretations"; others were weakened by their authors' "inability to leave non-significant results alone." But the saddest aspect, concluded Anderson, was "the failure of the project to provide any progress in the area of effects" of television on children.[4] Recalling the 1961 assessment of Schramm, Lyle, and Parker ("For some children, under some conditions, some television is harmful"), he summed up his indictment:

> Eleven years and at least one million dollars later we are still at that level of sophistication. Where are the answers to the types of children affected, the conditions under which they are affected, the content which is effective? Why did the committee fund research dealing with questions already a decade out of date?[5]

Those directly involved in the research were willing to provide the press with their own summaries of what the research really meant. Professor Robert Liebert told *The New York Times* the studies quite clearly demonstrated "that watching violence in a television context can instigate aggressive behavior in children"[6]—certainly a more clear-cut conclusion than the Committee had been able to agree upon.

Publications serving or focusing on television had fairly predictable reactions. *Broadcasting* magazine, having already misreported the release of the Surgeon General's study with the glowing headline: "Violence on Air and in Life: No Clear Link,"[7] carried an editorial following Pastore's hearings in order to attack the proposal for a violence profile. Scorning this endeavor—"to protect the young against a contagion of hostilities"—*Broadcasting* argued that a violence profile "would in the end lead only to the enfeeblement of television." Pastore's suggestion, it was argued, was based on a million dollar study that was "largely inconclusive."[8]

TV Guide published a three-part series by Edith Efron entitled "A Million Dollar Misunderstanding." Ms. Efron argued that each of the scientific caveats expressed in the Committee's Report—problems of definition, measurement techniques, and research design—was sufficient "to wipe out the significance of much of the research."

> The authors conclude, cautiously, . . . that you can produce either "antisocial" or "prosocial" responses, depending on "the opportunities offered in the experiment." Which is a very courteous way of saying that researchers can manufacture the results they want.[9]

Ms. Efron singled out the press for criticism:

> [T]he press "corrected" its original error by overcompensating, and fell hook, line and sinker for the "truth seeker vs. network prostitute" interpretation of the controversy. It never realized it was being used as a bull horn by a particular intellectual faction and that powerful arguments existed on the other side.[10]

Echoing *Broadcasting's* editorials, Ms. Efron concluded her series:

> You are now going to be presented with a "Violence Index." It will make most people yawn and tune in to *Mission Impossible*. But it will throw others into a panic because they'll assume that there would be no "Violence Index" without proof that TV violence is dangerous to young viewers. Be advised that the "Violence Index" has only one real meaning: it is a non-solution to a nonproved problem produced by a noninvestigation of a nonresolved controversy over a nondefined threat to nonidentifiable people.[11]

Among other journalists, Jack Anderson seized upon Dr. Monroe Lefkowitz' attack on the Report as a key to its weakness. Aggrieved that the members of the Committee had found fault with his research even as they gave it signal prominence, Lefkowitz had written a bitter letter to Senator Pastore. Picked up and widely publicized in Anderson's column, it contained damning charges that the Report's conclusions were not only hedged by erroneous statements but in fact were "potentially damaging to children and society."[12] These protests were sufficient to cause Anderson to conclude that a "scientific backlash" had occurred. It also prompted the press to take a second look at the Report. *Newsweek,* having begun to sense the importance of the Surgeon General's findings in Morgenstern's earlier article on film violence, came out with a follow-up a month later:

> Now . . . there is emerging a dramatically different picture of what the Surgeon General's study actually unearthed—and how those revelations were drawn up for public display. In tones of outrage and disgust, many of the forty psychologists and social scientists who did the original research for the project are claiming that their findings did, in fact, establish a clear and direct link between TV violence and youthful, antisocial behavior. In essence, the dissenters level a four-count indictment. They charge that: (1) the membership of the advisory committee of twelve scientists which analyzed the violence research for the Surgeon General was rigged to favor the television industry; (2) the 260-page report produced by the advisory committee softened the findings contained in the five volumes of original research upon which the report was based; (3) the nineteen-page summary of the full report which was first released to the press was made even more equivocal than the report itself; (4) the media inadvertently misread the summary in such a way as to largely absolve video violence of any significant effect on youngsters.[13]

Others were more supportive of the Surgeon General's Committee. In a piece for the *Washington Post,* Henry Mitchell wrote:

> The report was issued in January. It consists of five volumes of research papers and a 300-page summary which I have made a stab at. I cannot see why it is controversial—or at least why there should be any great doubt what its meaning is:
> "We have evidence, admittedly not massive or conclusive or irrefutable, that violence on television can and does cause aggressiveness in children's behavior. We don't know how serious this is, but we are worried about it.
> "We think a great deal more attention should be given to this whole subject of television violence than has been done in the past, and while we do not recommend panic or suggest blaming television for the ills of society, still we have an uneasy feeling that a daily climate of pictured violence on television may be hazardous to the nation's emotional health."
> That is not what the report says. Those are my words and they express my own estimate of what the report means.[14]

A number of professionals who had not been involved in the Surgeon General's effort pointed to weaknesses in the Report but agreed that its overall value outweighed specific shortcomings. Dr. Timothy Meyer of the University of Massachusetts believed that a stronger, better-coordinated research strategy would have produced more coherent results. Some of the studies, he felt, were of questionable quality, and others represented no advance in knowledge. But he found Gerbner's content analysis to be "a compilation of useful and reliable data, providing researchers, critics, and the public with an accurate assessment of various quantitative and qualitative dimensions of violent television content."[15] Meyer also pointed to the usefulness of those studies probing the perceptions of persons involved in producing television shows and of the laboratory experiments measuring aggressive reactions.[16]

George Comstock, former senior research coordinator for the Surgeon General's Committee, wrote a perceptive paper for the Rand Corporation in May 1972 entitled "Television Violence: Where the Surgeon General's Study Leads." Agreeing that the Report was "undeniably embellished with qualifications," Comstock nevertheless felt that the Report offered "a broad but pertinent and scientifically and socially meaningful conclusion that can command consensus."[17] Since the Report had satisfactorily—if not fully—resolved the "causal hypothesis," it was now time to give research priority to its implications. Comstock urged that future research use panel studies and field experiments both to further validate the link between laboratory findings and ordinary life and to further analyze the "a) social and psychological processes which have an influence or mediating role in televised violence's effect on aggressiveness; b) mitigating conditions; c) prosocial effects of televised violence; and d) prosocial influences of television."[18]

Future policy studies should focus on discovering how to produce more desirable television, how to release competition's hold on programming, and how to construct meaningful everyday action from what social science can learn. While stressing the need for further research, Comstock concluded:

> The evidence at present—despite the attention given here to the importance of further confirmation—clearly indicates that televised violence contributes to aggressiveness among the young, and therefore constitutes a significant and serious problem for our society—and probably for other modernized societies as well. Our society has pioneered in the study of this issue. It now has the opportunity to pioneer in its solution.[19]

Yet even Dr. Comstock's analysis was subjected to misinterpretation. *Broadcasting* headed its account: "Dr. Comstock has second thoughts on violence study." An editorial in the same issue concluded:

> Now that Dr. Comstock's own re-evaluation of the original report has been circularized, it is more evident than ever that the government has no business spending any more money to follow up a study that, despite its huge scope and expense, is still subject to changing interpretations.[20]

This prompted Dr. Rubinstein to comment wryly:

> I should perhaps take some comfort in the fact that Broadcasting Magazine is still sufficiently apprehensive about the impact of our study to report, distort, and editorialize on Dr. Comstock's paper and to urge no more studies.[21]

One of the more detailed reviews, written by Leo Bogart and published in the Winter 1972–73 issue of *Public Opinion Quarterly,* was entitled "Warning: The Surgeon General Has Determined That TV Violence is Moderately Dangerous To Your Child's Mental Health." He cautioned against being "too critical of the style or internal consistency of a government report prepared by civil servants under tremendous time pressure or of technical reports written by academic researchers for submission in fulfillment of contracts rather than for publication in scholarly journals,"[22] and concluded that "the eclectic and interdisciplinary character of the studies, the heterogeneity of methods and theoretical orientations make the report a noteworthy exemplar of applied social research."[23] Still, Bogart had reservations about substance. Common sense and prior research had already shown that "communications leave effects and that violence is bad rather than good."[24] Only a few of the twenty-six studies contained in the Surgeon General's Report added to this knowledge. Thus, Bogart queried, "Was this study really necessary?" He answered his question:

> [T]he issue should never have been made one of "proving" a case against TV violence, or failing to prove it. The legal analogy simply does not apply to science, where we come ever closer to an elusive truth by a constant reexamination of the evidence, where exceptions are more interesting than generalizations, and where the quality of almost any study is to be judged not only by its findings but by the new questions it presents.[25]

Perhaps the most important single reaction to the Surgeon General's inquiry came from the Surgeon General himself. Jesse

Steinfeld, who had inherited a controversial project he did not initiate and surely must have wished at times he could forget, not only endorsed the Report officially, but continued to call for action long after there was any official obligation for his doing so. Increasingly isolated from HEW policymaking, Steinfeld resigned as Surgeon General in January 1973. Out of office, he wrote in the May 1973 issue of *Reader's Digest:*

> These studies—and scores of similar ones—make it clear to me that the relationship between televised violence and antisocial behavior is sufficiently proved to warrant immediate remedial action. Indeed, the time has come to be blunt: We can no longer tolerate the present high level of televised violence that is put before children in American homes.[26]

Steinfeld urged American parents to demand better television fare for their children by directly contacting the networks, the National Association of Broadcasters, Congress, and the FCC.

To what appeared to be an increasing pressure from the critics that television violence must be reduced, a plaguing question remained: under what authority? Robert Lewis Shayon, writing in *Saturday Review,* saw only two choices to the latter question:

> [T]he findings of even a tentative causal link between TV violence and aggression represents the crossing of a Rubicon. Further research may strengthen the evidence of that link. The plague must be arrested, and it can be if the networks, to avoid destructive competition for audiences, somehow agree to deescalate violence collectively. . . . All else failing, the nation will commit the ultimate violence upon itself by the act of censorship.[27]

11

THE GOVERNMENT'S
HESITANT RESPONSE

Senator Pastore had reason to believe that his hearings on the Surgeon General's Advisory Committee Report had imbued all parties with a new sense of need and purpose. The Surgeon General had asserted, on the basis of the Report, that the television industry "should be put on notice." FCC Chairman Burch pledged to keep the networks' "feet to the fire" to remedy their programming practices and to do better by their most impressionable constituency, America's children.[1]

Yet, in terms of specific next steps, only one line of action seemed especially promising: Senator Pastore's proposal for a violence index or profile. It was thought to have several values. It would track overall levels and patterns of television violence according to standardized criteria; this would permit a less random answer to the core question: How much violence do we actually get over our TV sets? Such an annual measurement of "tele-violence" would be helpful to parents and even useful to sponsors who wished to avoid the association of their products with programs of high violence content. Finally, an annual report from an objective source might also, some thought, help to raise writers' standards, especially for children's programs.

When asked for their reactions to the idea at the March hearings, representatives of the television networks responded cautiously. His specific response, said NBC President Julian Goodman, would depend on what the measuring device looked like and how it was used. But he was not opposed in principle to measuring television violence content.[2] Elton Rule, president of ABC, concurred. In answer to Senator Baker's questioning he explained:

> [W]e certainly have no objection to the overall thought. I would like to know more of the mechanics before I said yes. . . . But we would be quite willing to investigate, to discuss, in whatever forum, the possibility of such a move and would approach it with an open mind.[3]

Most supporters of the proposal stressed that the actual monitoring should be carried out by a nongovernmental agency. Two foundation presidents, Orville G. Brim, Jr., of Russell Sage Foundation, and Lloyd Morrisett of the Markle Foundation, had already offered tentative support for this effort.[4] Senator Pastore had no quarrel with involving outsiders, but he was anxious that responsibility for the development and implementation of such a profile be specifically assigned. Thus he pressed that responsibility on the Secretary of Health, Education and Welfare in cooperation with the FCC. At the completion of the March hearings, he wrote Elliot Richardson:

> As you know, just as critical as the answer the Report gave the question of televised violence and its impact on children is the need for action to implement its findings. As was stated during the hearings, failure to act is an acquiescence in the continuation of the present level of television violence entering American homes.
>
> Your Department is, of course, the principal agency of Government responsible for the physical and mental health of our citizens. We are, therefore, requesting that your Department proceed in consultation with the Federal Communications Commission to develop a measurement for violence on television so that a report can be submitted annually to this Committee on the level of violence entering American homes.[5]

Richardson's reply was qualified. He reported that the NIMH staff was "actively involved in discussing with experts in the field" various aspects of the proposal and that a two-year research grant on the subject had been made to Dr. George Gerbner of the Annenberg School of Communications. But, Richardson cautioned, "very frankly, an assessment of the 'state of the art' is required before developing a 'violence index' of the scope you have suggested." He promised a report, after further consultation with experts, providing "our best judgment on the feasibility of developing such an index."[6]

In June, NIMH convoked a "special consultation" to discuss the violence measurement idea. Meeting with staff of that agency and the FCC were government and university researchers as well as representatives of private foundations having an interest in the subject. The report of this conference indicated keen awareness of the delicate nature of the problem being explored.

> Participants rejected the idea that an index should be developed for regulatory use; there was considerable concern that the mere existence of a measure . . . might imply if not actually be a move toward regulation.[7]

There was further concern about the nature of the violence index:

> The participants underlined hazards involved in any simple frequency count of violent acts . . . the need was *not* for a single violence index or measure, but for a multidimensional "profile" which would characterize televised violence on as many dimensions as possible.[8]

There was also discussion of the need for studies of viewer perceptions of violence in addition to content analysis. And, with a degree of optimism, the group reported:

> [A] major conclusion of the session was that if an index is to be useful in enlarging program choice, an adversary relationship between the industry and those developing the index must be avoided. There was some feeling that the time had come when the industry might welcome some general guidelines.[9]

The conference was able to summarize seven recommendations. These were:

> —A profile of televised violence should be developed rather than a simple index or measure of its frequency or level. . . .

> —The development of such a profile is feasible. Research is still needed to solve problems of content and design, but the profile can, and should, evolve as the research is carried out and not wait for its total completion.

> —The profile should be seen as an instrument for public and industry education and as providing an information base for constructive influence to widen and improve programming. It should not be for regulation or program restriction.

> —The profile should be developed, maintained, and reported on outside of

both the TV industry and the federal Government. . . .

—The profile should operate in a context in which alternative programming is encouraged and illustrated and there are rewards for broadening and improving the range of interests and behaviors portrayed, as well as negative sanctions for exceeding certain bounds.

—The profile should draw on and incorporate ongoing research on the behavioral effects of viewing and provide insights for researchers; it should not be allowed to become a static measuring device.

—There are several models for an appropriate institutional arrangement for planning and development of the profile outside of government and industry that are available for the consideration of planners and social scientists; this should make it possible to begin work soon so that the momentum created by the work of the Surgeon General's Advisory Committee and congressional hearings on its report will not be lost.[10]

Secretary Richardson was still cautious when he reported to Senator Pastore in July, declaring:

Our staff and consultants feel strongly that an index of the incidence of TV violence is of only limited usefulness. A more constructive profile of TV violence could be developed, made up of indices of a number of significant dimensions—level, frequency, characteristics of those involved, their motivations, whether the violence is explained or not, audience perception of violence, and its short and long-term effects on various kinds of viewers.[11]

Richardson concluded:

Upon development of the profile it would be disseminated periodically to the Congress, the Federal Communications Commission, this Department, and other interested organizations, thus helping government and industry to fulfill their responsibilities to the American people.[12]

Senator Pastore wished to know who was to assume further responsibility for the additional research and when a report on that research could be expected. The secretary responded that HEW's intention was "to leave the planning and actual maintenance of a television violence profile to extra-governmental institutions who might be supported under existing grant program authority." As to additional research, he pointed once more to NIMH support of Dr. George Gerbner's continuing work, which "would contribute one of several needed dimensions to the profile."[13]

Gerbner and his colleagues cautioned that the indicators of violence were "not statistical findings in themselves," but were instead "convenient illustrators" of the levels and kinds of television violence. Believing the concept of an index was being interpreted too narrowly, Gerbner changed the title of his regular reports on his research to "The Violence-Profile," four months after the original report was issued, to emphasize "the greater range of measures and dimensions reflected in it."[14]

Ironically, as HEW placed increasing reliance on Gerbner's research effort, the White House Office of Telecommunications Policy began to circulate criticisms of this effort. In June 1972, OTP staff member Bruce Owen produced an analysis which faulted Gerbner's approach largely on grounds that it was misleading and subject to manipulation.

In order to produce a single, numerical measure of TV violence, Owen felt that Gerbner had settled on a faulty formula whose factors were not only "dimensionless," but arbitrarily chosen and weighted. Moreover, "useful information on the extent of violence on television must take into account the *nature* of the violence in terms of its effects on people. Mere counting is interesting, but the aggregation of counts into a 'violence index' is extremely misleading."[15] Such an exercise, he stated, "involves adding apples and oranges."[16]

Owen acknowledged that a "measurable phenomenon" called "violence on television" might well exist, but, he concluded, "the proper course of action is first to understand its effects, and then to measure [violence] in methodologically acceptable ways in terms of the psychological or sociological effects which matter."[17]

Dr. Gerbner replied: "All indexes are by definition composed of 'apples and oranges;' that is why they are useful to those who are primarily interested in 'fruit.' "[18] He continued: "It is of course true that all acts of violence are not the same. But that does not eliminate the need for crime statistics or casualty reports."[19]

In Gerbner's judgment:

> There is basic confusion running through the [Owen] report. It is confusion between research on the effects of violence and the reliable determination of aspects of the clear and unambiguous incidence of violent action in dramatic presentations. The latter can provide the basis for research on the role of the symbolic functions of dramatic violence in real-life conceptions and behavior, but not the other way around.
>
> To say that "the proper course of action is first to understand its effects, and then to measure it in methodologically acceptable ways in terms of the

psychological or sociological *effects* which matter" is a prime example of this confusion. It is like saying that we must first understand why people feel the way they do before we can study the elements that compose the environment in which they live. In fact, a scientific study starts with the determination of these elements and not with presumed social, moral or policy effects of unknown or vaguely specified messages.[20]

In response to Senator Pastore's request for a time schedule, Secretary Richardson suggested that depending upon the outcome of additional necessary research, including the Gerbner studies, "the development of a meaningful television violence profile will take from two to four years." Richardson promised to keep the Senate "apprised of developments in this field as we become aware of them."[21]

Thus, many months after Pastore had put the ball in HEW's court, it became clear that the Department had passed it to the researchers. And, as always, the social scientists and communications researchers who were asked what to do about a policy proposal suggested the need for more research. Yet there was a signal difference this time. The consensus among the experts who had reviewed the matter at the HEW meeting was that the violence profile "can and should evolve as the research is carried out and not wait for its total completion."

Throughout 1972, NIMH officials reported "a high level of interest in this subject in the scientific community."[22] In fact, few research proposals were submitted to the agency the results of which were likely to be building blocks for a violence profile. Why had not the social scientists manifested their interest by submitting proposals? One answer might be that the evidence of interest on the other side—the government side—seemed largely verbal. Aside from convoking the "special consultancy," and subsequent informal conversations with the Social Science Research Council, there was no public notice issued that the Department was devoting high priority to research on television and social behavior.

By early 1973, both Assistant Secretary DuVal and Surgeon General Steinfeld had left their government posts. Secretary Richardson was soon shifted to the Defense Department and later Justice, before his celebrated resignation over the Watergate investigation. At NIMH, Dr. Eli Rubinstein had gone to the State University of New York at Stony Brook; most of his associates, recruited for the television research project, had also left. More important than this exodus was the fact that HEW was signalling its declining interest in the matter by reductions in the research budget. The NIMH budget for all behavioral science research dropped from $20 million in fiscal year 1969 to $16 million for fiscal year 1973 and again for fiscal year 1974. Dr. David Pearl, Chief of the Behavioral Sciences Research Branch, indicated that neither the television profile nor research on television generally had been designated as a high priority area.

While FCC Chairman Dean Burch did not meet his announced schedule of convening a panel of experts to talk about children and television in May of 1972, the Commission did hold a three-day public panel in October devoted to specific children's programming issues. It was, in the dour opinion of the *Washington Post*, "an endless bull session that, like all endless bull sessions, came to no conclusions."[23] Network spokesmen maintained that children's television was better than ever; citizens' action groups argued that it was getting worse.

FCC staff studies, not released to the public, tended to support the contention that official action was needed. An analysis of trends in diversity of content over a twenty-year period concluded that the periodic swings in children's television fare were directly related to publicly stated protests from policymakers. Matching up and down trends of violence with activities of the FCC or congressional committees over the years, the staff document concluded:

> It is possible to hypothesize that without pressure, or encouragement, and without "holding their feet to the fire" the broadcast industry tends to take the well worn path while writing off the child audience as captive viewers.[24]

In an April 1973 interview published in *TV Guide*, the FCC chairman who had earlier evidenced such concern about televised violence also expressed puzzlement as to what the FCC should do about it. He said:

> I have very mixed feelings on this whole question of sex, violence and profanity on television. Violence has come to the fore because of the Surgeon General's report and all the controversy surrounding the findings. The report said in effect, "We have some tentative conclusions, but we particularly urge a great deal more research, more definitions." For example, the report

argues that violence in an appropriate setting is not necessarily disturbing. A case in point which the Surgeon General gave me in a conversation was of a cowboy show in which you see somebody fire a gun, somebody falls dead, and the next happy scene is of the hero riding off into the sunset. Apparently he [the Surgeon General] would feel differently if you instead showed a funeral for the man who was killed, the widow and her crying children, and all that. This would be different. It would show the consequences of violence. And perhaps he's right. For myself, I don't know. Is Mickey Mouse running over an opponent with a steam engine and the opponent afterward puffing up to normality and running off—is that "violence"? I don't know. Do children relate that to "violence"? I don't know.[25]

Senator Pastore and his Subcommittee held hearings in February 1973 on a range of communications policy matters. Children's television was only briefly mentioned. Chairman Burch again stated the need for "greater diversity in children's programming," including special afternoon programs directed to school-age children. He also stressed the need for correcting present commercial practices in children's television. While he felt that "the three industries involved, broadcasting, advertising, and programming, are making some good faith efforts to respond to public criticism," he agreed that this "does not get the commission off the hook. . . . We are considering rule making or policy statements or a combination of both in all the areas I have mentioned. The staff is working up option papers, and decisions should be forthcoming by late spring."[26]

In fact, by year's end, the Federal Communications Commission had still taken no action. Yet the issue of television's potentially adverse effects on children would not die. At the FCC as in other arenas, the Surgeon General's Report seemed to have reinforced convictions that something should be done. But the question of what to do remained tricky. Even for those Commissioners who thought the new research clearly showed TV violence to have potentially harmful effects, that research clearly did *not* show the way to specific rules about program content—even if the First Amendment was thought to permit such rules.

In December 1973, Chairman Burch stated that the Commission would probably take action in early 1974. That action, he suggested, would be in two parts: a new FCC rule limiting the number of commercial minutes, and perhaps the kind of commercials, to be permitted during the presentation of children's programs; and second, a policy statement aimed at encouraging net-works and individual stations to provide more and better programs for children in the pre- and post-school hours, and the early evening.

This two-pronged approach, Burch suggested, would be evolutionary but the most sensible course the FCC could presently follow. It would get at what he—along with ACT—obviously believes to be the most serious problems regarding television's role in the lives of children: over-commercialization and lack of quality programming.[27]

Meanwhile, with Senator Pastore's image constantly hovering in the background, NIMH in the late summer of 1973 awarded a three-year, $150,000 grant to the Social Science Research Council to carry out two mandates: first, to specify what new research was needed to hone the results of earlier research to finer conclusions; and second, to explore the promise and problems of developing a violence profile. Chaired by Professor Stephen Withey of the University of Michigan Institute for Social Research, the SSRC committee delegated these mandates to a number of prominent researchers in the area of television and children. The new committee met for the first time in October 1973 to address specifically the issue of the development of a violence profile. But Dr. Withey cautioned there was no certainty that the Committee would endorse the idea or come up with an action plan for carrying it out.

Senator Pastore, still convinced of the value of prodding, wrote another letter on October 8, 1973—to the new HEW Secretary, Caspar Weinberger. Noting his abundant correspondence with HEW over the past year and a half, he once again patiently repeated:

> The [Senate] Committee is, of course, vitally concerned with all aspects of children's programming, including the progress of the violence profile. I would, therefore, appreciate a report on the current status of efforts to develop the profile, and an estimate of when the Committee may expect it to be completed.[28]

As the year drew to an end, Weinberger sent Pastore his reply. Detailing the eleven research projects initiated or continued during the past fiscal year as well as the grant to the Social Science Research Council, Weinberger also stressed NIMH's continued support of Dr. Gerbner's content analyses. In Weinberger's opinion:

> This content analysis approach, broadened to encompass a number of additional dimensions and linked with viewers' perceptions of violence and its effects . . . could provide a substantial advance in the development of a violence profile.[29]

However, it appeared that the secretary was not yet willing to face the violence-profile issue head on. His letter concluded:

> NIMH staff and consultants continue to judge that the development of an adequate multidimensional violence profile will require a minimum of two to three additional years.[30]

To keep up the pressure, Senator Pastore let it be known that he intended to hold another round of hearings. They would, according to his deputy Nicholas Zapple, probably be held sometime in the spring—on the fifth anniversary of the senator's original request for the Surgeon General's inquiry.

12

THE INDUSTRY'S RESPONSE

Although the government could drag out its deliberations, the broadcast industry could not leave the airwaves empty while debating the amount and character of televised violence. Here, where program ratings are a daily reality and violence an unchallenged drawing card, the Surgeon General's Report would face its severest test.

Broadcasters greeted the announcement of the findings with conspicuous silence. But at the Senate hearings two months later, their testimony was vaguely supportive. Under Pastore's prodding, the three network heads found themselves on the spot. Julian Goodman, president of the National Broadcasting Company, declared that his network accepted the responsibility which the central conclusion of the Advisory Committee Report had placed upon him and his colleagues. He noted that NBC was seeking "to learn more about the subject and, at the same time, avoid programs that could have undesirable effects on children." But when Goodman felt obliged to add that "an accurate definition of the problem is essential to our search for a solution,"[1] Pastore bridled. He thought Goodman's stress on the need for further study was "too heavy" and pointed out that all seven members of the Advisory Committee who testified had agreed with Surgeon General

113

Steinfeld that "the data are sufficient to justify action."[2]

John Schneider, president of the CBS Broadcast Group, testified that the Report ". . . tells me that anyone seeking easy answers to questions about the effects on society of the portrayal of violence on television will be disappointed."[3] Pastore responded that network officials were relying on loopholes to avoid the central thrust of the Report. He had been much impressed, the senator said pointedly, "when I asked your Dr. Klapper and Dr. Coffin, who represents NBC, how they felt about this, and both of them agreed with the Surgeon General. . . . They took a position that something needs to be done and it ought to be done soon."[4]

Elton Rule, president of the American Broadcasting Company, was the most forthright of the three network heads about the need for action. Like Goodman and Schneider, he pointed out that "many questions remain to be answered," but he agreed that the Report's finding of a relationship between televised violence and increased aggressive behavior in some children "represents a substantial advance in our knowledge, and the industry and we at ABC will have to weigh its implications very seriously."[5] Enumerating the reforms ABC planned to initiate during the coming season, Rule stressed that the Surgeon General's Report had reinforced the network's "early determinations" and had made it clear to broadcasters that they "must be even more responsive" in managing their program planning. Pastore graciously accepted the statement as it stood, offering congratulations for Rule's willingness to incorporate the Report's findings into ABC's fall scheduling.

One disquieting cloud over this apparent amity was the scant coverage given by network news to the hearings. When Dr. Eli Rubinstein asked a network reporter why the opening day's testimony—which had drawn a large crowd and received modest coverage in the print media—was practically ignored on the television evening news, he was told that word had come from New York not to put much emphasis on the hearings.[6] Pastore, evidently accustomed to this silent treatment, wryly commented to the television camera crews present in the committee room that they were wasting their time. The Canadian Broadcasting Corporation, on the other hand, produced a one-hour documentary, "The Question of Television Violence," based on the Pastore hearings. It has been shown to groups of interested persons but not on the airwaves in this country.

The Surgeon General's Report appeared to have little influence on the industry's decisions for the 1972–73 season. Despite the assurances of the network heads, critics noted that previous programs with a high incidence of violence remained on the new fall schedules.[7] According to one critic, a few initial episodes of the new season's offerings began to show "the real face of violence, ugly and frightening," but those aspects quickly receded and "TV's standard portrayal of brutality as glamorous, exciting, sometimes 'artistic' " took over once again.[8] By June, the conclusions of the critics were reinforced by a detailed content analysis produced by George Gerbner and Larry Gross, *The Violence Profile No. 5.* This latest report was an extension of their earlier work but also represented a new effort to develop a set of cultural indicators that would trace trends in media content and their effects upon viewers.

Defining violence as "the overt expression of physical force compelling action against one's will on pain of being hurt or killed, or actually hurting or killing,"[9] Drs. Gerbner and Gross found that while the 1972 composite index of dramatic violence on prime-time network television remained below the 1967–68 levels, still eight out of ten programs and nine out of every ten cartoons contained some violence.

> The actual prevalence of violence . . . did not change since these studies began in 1967. The rate of violence episodes also remained about 5 per program and 8 per hour (17 per cartoon hour).[10]

What had declined was the percentage of leading characters involved in violence—a drop from 73 percent to 58 percent—and the proportion involved in killing—from 19 percent to 10 percent.[11]

> However, the ratio of victimization (the margin of victims over perpetrators of violence) rose to a new high, and struck particularly hard at women and non-whites.[12]

The fact that increasingly more television characters suffer than inflict violence, the two researchers argued, "cultivates a margin of fear and demonstrates a structure of power that television viewers may project upon reality."[13]

Gerbner and Gross found that those programs which had been continued from 1971 were more violent, but those programs started in 1972 were less violent than previous seasons.[14] NBC's programs were the most violent of the three networks. ABC, despite President Rule's assurances to Pastore, also showed an increase. CBS was down from the previous year and least violent of the three.[15]

As a beginning effort in measuring effects, the researchers found "the first clear evidence of a relationship between television viewing and conceptions of social reality that conform to the world of television but contrast with real life."[16] In response to questioning, significantly more heavy (four plus hours a day) than light (two or less hours a day) viewers overestimated the percentage of real-life violent crimes as well as the danger of their personal involvement. Gerbner and Gross suggested that heavy television viewing had strongly influenced this exaggerated picture of reality among heavy viewers.

Industry officials were skeptical of Gerbner's effort to develop a violence profile. In a lengthy article in the winter 1972–73 issue of the *Journal of Broadcasting* entitled "Rating Television Programming for Violence: A Comparison of Five Surveys," NBC vice-president of research planning, Thomas Coffin, who had been a member of the Surgeon General's Advisory Committee, and NBC's director of research projects, Sam Tuchman, compared Gerbner's analyses to other violence rating systems. They concluded that there were substantial discrepancies. First, a sizable number of network programs—especially those which tended to be nonviolent—were excluded from measurement in the Gerbner studies. Second, Gerbner's results indicated a higher incidence of violence because his definitions went beyond "commonsense notions" to include accidents, humorous violence, and acts of nature.[17]

Drs. Coffin and Tuchman objected that:

> The root of the problem would seem to be not with the Gerbner studies per se, but with the way his figures have been put to use and cited by readers who ignore the stated limitations.[18]

Rating a program for violent content serves as an implicit warning to parents that the program might be harmful to their children. Gerbner's data, designed to provide a series of sociological indicators, were being used as "violence ratings."

Coffin and Tuchman concluded:

. . . [W]ithout a valid understanding of the *kinds* of television violence that cause or contribute to particular kinds of undesirable behavior, the construction of a television index may be both "fruitless and misleading" because it is the effects of television violence rather than the arithmetic of episodes that should be measured. . . . Thus a vital step in developing such systems is research designed to discriminate between "harmful" and "harmless" violence. This would ensure that such systems will focus on the real area of social concern: *harmful* depictions of violence.[19]

Dr. Gerbner and two colleagues, replying in the same issue of *Journal of Broadcasting,* claimed there was confusion in the Coffin-Tuchman analysis. They argued that an essential component of any rating system had to be the systematic, objective, and reliable inventory of the relevant aspects of television content.

To weight slapstick violence less heavily than serious dramatic violence may seem to be conventional wisdom, but in fact it is scientifically unacceptable. Humor may be the best vehicle for the effective cultivation of certain definitions, images and attitudes.[20]

As a parting shot, Gerbner and his colleagues maintained that no one could argue that there is no information on the effects of violence.

. . . [T]he reports of the Surgeon General's Committee (of which Dr. Coffin was a member) have indicated a sufficiently strong relationship between violent tendencies and the sheer frequency of exposure to *any* TV violence to suggest a public health problem.[21]

As the 1973 season got underway, critics found little evidence of change except for a few family situation programs which, interestingly, reached the top ten ratings. Washington *Star* critic Bernie Harrison summed up his discontent:

Commercial TV has really been asking for it this new season. There are at least a score of police and private eye dramas and in all of these violence is one of the essentials. In the competition, shocking detail is an inevitable trend.[22]

Anthony La Camera, of the *Boston Herald American,* commented:

There is a growing stench about prime-time programming that may well lead to civic outcries for a congressional or FCC deodorant. Too much of the programming is dehumanizing, desensitizing, cynical and depressing.[23]

And Claire Berman wrote in *New York* magazine:

> I have just spent several weekday mornings and two very long weekends
> watching this season's schedule of shows for the young, and let me tell you,
> I'd settle for funny. Or tasteful. Or original. I'd prefer educational but I'd
> settle for entertaining. Because what children are being offered this season
> is largely a rehash of the reprehensible TV fare that's been given them in the
> past. Inane cartoon versions of adult situation comedies and adventure sto-
> ries predominate. . . .[24]

There were signs that network officials were sensitive to the
issue. Herminio Traviesas, NBC vice-president for broadcast
standards, claimed his network was ruthlessly eliminating "gratuitous" violence: "At every stage of a show—from script to rough cut
to final editing—the producers have to prove that a violent act is
vital to the story."[25]

Paradoxically, the network that according to Gerbner had
moved the farthest struck the most adamant posture in resisting
outside pressures for change. CBS Television's President Robert
D. Wood defended controversial programming as in keeping with
his network's commitment "to participate in the present." "Part of
being fully responsive to our public," he argued, "is to make sure
that we do not allow a small, vocal, and, at times, highly organized
minority to determine what can be seen on your television set."[26]

Still, certain changes appeared to be the order of the day. All
three networks created a special Vice-President in Charge of Children's Programming. They also called on child experts, television
experts, and advertising executives to join together in discussions
concerning programming.[27] CBS announced in June 1973 the appointment of two specialists in educational planning for children
"to act as advisors in the development, planning and concepts of
quality programming for children, not only for scheduled Saturday
shows, but also for specials, mini-series and all other children's
programs."[28] When specific problems arose, these educators
would be requested to assemble an interdisciplinary group to
guide programmers "in insuring children a learning experience
combined with entertainment, one that will be helpful in their
mental growth and development of judgment and moral values."[29]

An interesting liason between educators and broadcasters
took place under the auspices of the Kaiser Broadcasting Company. This company, with stations in six major cities, hired Profes-

sors George Gerbner, Ithiel de Sola Pool, and Eleanor Maccoby to act as consultants for youth programming. Beyond reviewing the existing cartoons, they designed and helped initiate "Snippets"— one-minute educational commercials inserted between the cartoons—which contain material stressing "How To's" and other prosocial messages.[30]

One caustic dissenter, Edith Efron, writing for *TV Guide*, "The Children's Crusade That Failed," maintained that changes intended to make a "Saturday morning Golden Age" had "boomeranged."

> In capitulating to the pressures of the antiviolence campaigners, the networks gutted the basic nucleus of storytelling, lost all purpose and coherence and filled the conceptual void with canned yoks. The result: programming that was nonviolent but still nauseated many adults who saw it.[31]

Ms. Efron emphasized that only 9 percent of total child viewing is confined to the Saturday morning hours on which the networks were concentrating their reforms. Others also pointed out that during 1972, 85 percent of children's afternoon viewing in the top fifty markets was not directed to network shows but to adult programming broadcast by independent stations. Getting at the sources of violence programming was not to be a simple mission. The most directly measurable results so far have been accomplished by citizen action. A spokesman for the parent group, Action for Children's Television (ACT), has claimed:

> We are beginning to find that parents, teachers, pediatricians, and psychiatrists are much more aware than they were before of the impact of TV on the lives of children and are beginning to think of ways of dealing with it.[32]

The potential for this sort of enterprise was demonstrated in the fall of 1973 when four citizen groups in Los Angeles joined to bring pressure against the independent station KTTV to remove certain heavily violent programs and to issue cautionary warnings when broadcasting others. The threat to challenge its license renewal brought a promise of compliance from the station. In San Francisco, a parents' group has similarly pushed for a "children's bill of rights" from local stations, urging a special survey of needs for an age group which comprises one-fourth of the Bay Area audience.

One irate citizen with more than usual clout is Leo Singer, president of the Miracle White detergent company. After watching a spate of gunplay on four commercial channels in Chicago, Singer withdrew $2 million of his firm's commercials from violent shows. Singer has declared war on "mind pollution" in dramatic terms:

> If one TV show featuring a bizarre crime has a one in 10,000,000 chance of giving some lunatic a new murderous idea, think what twenty shows do to the odds. Radio has made it successfully without violence; why can't TV? Do we value life so little in this country today that we put the entertainment of many above the life of one?[33]

At least one of the researchers for the Surgeon General's Report believes that citizen action is the best way to accomplish change without inviting government control. Dr. Robert Liebert has declared:

> The most potent, the smoothest way to change television is through even a small minority of citizens who give the impression that they are going to react negatively to content.[34]

Urging parents to write not to the networks but to the sponsors, Liebert concluded that:

> It doesn't take very many of those kinds of letters for the sponsors—whose money underlies all this—to tell the network: "I'm not so sure that I want to buy time with those cartoons."[35]

Liebert's proposal represents a somewhat different approach from those who urge that the best way of reducing violence and other pernicious influences on children's programming is to reduce or eliminate the commercials. This has become the focus of ACT's campaign. In 1970, ACT requested the FCC to require stations to air at least fourteen hours of children's programming a week and to bar all advertising on them. Four years later—after holding two sets of hearings, compiling seventy-two volumes of testimony from broadcasters, advertisers, and ordinary citizens, and receiving well over 100,000 letters—the FCC finally responded. On October 31, 1974, it issued its long-awaited report and policy statement. It declined to issue rules as ACT and others had urged, but instead suggested goals to be achieved through industry self-regulation regarding appropriate kinds and amounts of children's programs and appropriate kinds and amounts of commercials. Once more the Commission postponed any treatment of television violence, promising to report on its plans by the end of the year.

While protesting strongly about damage to program quality and profits, the networks have voluntarily cut commercials on the Saturday morning children's programs from sixteen to twelve minutes per hour—the ratio already applied to prime-time programming. Three major drug companies have switched hard-sell vitamin ads from the "children's hours" to programs later in the day.

Citizen power, many thoughtful observers agree, poses dangers. Militant minorities bringing pressure on timid broadcasters and advertisers could impose a culture control that would be crippling to creativity. Already there have been instances when classic movies were edited out of all reason to avoid stirring up ethnic protests. CBS-Television President Wood has a point in warning that this could bring a new kind of "wasteland."

But the answer is not a return to citizen apathy. The evidence is too strong that apathy breeds broadcaster indifference to the social effects of this powerful medium. The better course lies in establishing a more effective dialogue between the concerned citizen and the broadcast industry. It is too easy to ridicule efforts at improvement as "The Children's Crusade That Failed." Two facts remain constant amid all the claims and counterclaims: How to measure television's impact on society is a problem that will not go away; and how our children's minds are shaped continues to stir society's fundamental concern.

13

POSTSCRIPT , 1974

During the first week in April 1974, the Senate Subcommittee on Communications convened a second round of hearings on the subject of televised violence "to make sure," according to a sub-committee spokesman, "the issue doesn't die . . . for lack of interest or money. . . ."[1] Both the format and the witnesses closely resembled those of the 1972 hearings. In response to Senator Pastore's repeated question, "Is the situation improving, or are we wasting a lot of time and money?", government officials, television network executives, social scientists and concerned citizens offered testimony in support of frequently conflicting points of view. What was significantly different from the earlier hearings, however, was that the atmosphere of urgency now seemed diffused.

Committee members appeared to have lost interest in the subject. Both Chairman Pastore and Senator Baker were present for the opening day, but Baker soon left to inspect tornado damage in his home state of Tennessee. Although a few other members dropped by, Pastore was the only one to sit through all three days of testimony.

For the government, the FCC still had not adopted a policy statement on children's television programming and the two FCC members most concerned with the issue had left the commission.

123

Commissioner Nicholas Johnson's term had expired; Chairman Dean Burch had resigned to go into the White House as special counsel to the president. Although the new chairman, Richard Wiley, had assured Senator Pastore in March that he had "every intention of finishing this matter,"[2] he did not discuss what courses of action the Commission was considering. He refused to make public a six-month old "internal staff document" from the Commission's recently departed children's specialist, Elizabeth Roberts, but reluctantly allowed members of the committee staff to have a look at it.

Wiley had reported in response to an earlier House of Representatives query that 2.5 man years and about $45,000 had been spent on activities related to children's television during 1973.[3] Evidently, the results had not provoked any actions by the FCC.

Dr. Bertram Brown, Director of NIMH, reported to Pastore that the Social Science Research Council was making progress in its research to develop a violence profile. He assured the senator, ". . . we will have a working index within a year or two. I will see to that."[4] But he cautioned the committee that the use of such a profile could create a host of problems and posed the questions: "Would it be used by parents to determine acceptability of individual programs? Would producers use it to plan programs? Would it lead to lowering the number of violent events but perhaps increase the intensity and inhumanity of those that were left?"[5]

Dr. Brown cited other studies being supported by NIMH including: Dr. George Gerbner's continuing development of his profile of television programming; a project to develop an index of the medium's positive effects on mental health; a study of the causes and consequences of credibility in television news; and a study on the long-term effects of prosocial television programs. The director stressed that these studies represented an investment of $478,000 in 1973.[6] Further interrogation by Senator Pastore revealed that while the proposed HEW budget for the coming year would permit the continuation of projects already underway, no new studies could be supported.

Meanwhile, there were signs that the industry had made new reckonings. The release of the fall 1974 schedules showed, according to Les Brown of *The New York Times:* "The television networks next fall will cut back in programs that deal with violence and stress series concerned with family life and personal relationships. . . . According to industry sources, programs are being discarded for both rating inadequacy and in response to the recent hearings on television violence by the Senate Communications Committee."[7] *Broadcasting* reported that "the children's programming chiefs of all three networks forecast a virtual renaissance in that program category. A fair paraphrase of their declarations: Come this fall, the 'junk'—their own characterization of much that has come before—will be gone."[8] Each of the three networks would cancel some of the animated cartoons and substitute "live-action" shows using a greater variety of subject material. Each promised more sophisticated production techniques, prime-time script writers, "in-service training instructors" for film editors, and consultations with social scientists and communications scholars.[9] All three networks indicated that they would use prime-time early evening slots for quality children's specials.* According to Allen Ducovny, CBS-TV director of children's programming, such shows would "advance important prosocial messages, such as good behavior, good health habits, adhering to rules in the interest of safety, and showing respect."[10]

Network leaders conceded that all those steps amounted to a gamble and emphasized that they would not sacrifice entertainment to achieve education. George Heineman, NBC vice-president for children's programs, explained, "We're in the entertainment business, and no matter how we place our philosophical efforts, there will still be judgments on how well we entertain."[11] Still he predicted optimistically: "when all three networks get into balanced programming, meaning entertainment balanced with instructional and educational ideas, you'll find continued growth. It's another form of competition."[12]

The network heads arrived at the Senate hearings armed with evidence of their new zeal. John Schneider, president of CBS, assured Senator Pastore that "between the 1971–72 season and the current broadcast season, the number of acts of violence has declined by about 25 percent, based on an analysis by the CBS Office of Social Research."[13] Alfred R. Schneider, vice-president

---

*As of June 1974, court litigation had put the network claim to prime-time access in dispute and caused the cancellation of many of those program plans.

of ABC-TV told the subcommittee, "We have eliminated from cartoons the use of guns and knives as well as other highly imitable weapons."[14] He added that his network was continuing to carry out the pledge made before the subcommittee in 1972 that cartoon series depending on "action" without humor would be dropped from the network's schedule. Julian Goodman, chairman of the board of NBC, agreed that the relationship between television violence and aggressive behavior as reported by the Surgeon General's Committee "is now generally recognized."[15] But he expressed reservations about the usefulness of a violence profile. His network's system of program review, he explained, was to judge on a case-by-case basis whether a violent scene was an "acceptable part of the dramatic action that is not likely to be a model for violence."[16]

During their testimony, the network heads drew on reports from studies their research divisions had been conducting into the effects of televised violence on children. They included:

> From NBC: "Exposure to TV 'Violence' and Aggressive Behavior in Boys" by J. Ronald Milavsky and Berton Pekowsky, scheduled to be completed late 1975.
>
> From ABC: "Children's Reactions to Violent Material on Television" by Lieberman Research, Inc., a three-year study completed early 1974. "Studies of Children and Television" by Melvin Heller and Samuel Polsky, an ongoing study begun July 1970.
>
> From CBS: *Violence and Anti-Social Behavior,* by Stanley Milgram, published 1974.

These studies, costing up to $1 million each, employed techniques similar to those used by the researchers involved in the Surgeon General's inquiry: NBC's longitudinal study paralleled the correlational work done by Lefkowitz; ABC's studies, using written and oral psychological tests and direct observation, corresponded to some of Bandura's research. Their findings ranged from Stanley Milgram's statement that "if television is on trial, the judgment of this investigation must be the Scottish verdict: Not proven,"[17] to Heller and Polsky's conclusion that "violent crime is the result of multiple factors, and cannot be attributable to watching violent television programs."[18] The Lieberman study illuminated additional factors—such as the inclusion of humor, the extent to which a child identifies with a situation or character, or the type of violent act portrayed—which might produce changes in the stimulus to aggression.

Reviewing all this industry activity, Pastore was less caustic in his criticisms than he had been in previous years. "I hope there is as much improvement in the 1974–75 season as there has been this season," he told the network heads. Other non-industry witnesses were not persuaded. Dr. Eli Rubinstein, now appearing as a private citizen and professor at the State University of New York at Stony Brook, spoke pessimistically of responses to the effort he had shepherded. "So far as I know," he said, "there is no scientific evidence that the prevalence of violence on network dramatic programming has been significantly reduced in the past two years."[19] Rubinstein chided CBS for claiming "a significance beyond what was really warranted" by its Milgram study. Criticizing NIMH for research budget cutbacks that "will have a direct negative impact on extending knowledge in this area,"[20] he called instead for 1) a continuing research program to study ways of enhancing the value of television for children; 2) a distribution center for progress reports; and 3) a public advocate role to provide testimony on matters relating to children and violence.[21]

In conducting the hearings, Senator Pastore especially wanted to obtain a progress report on Dr. George Gerbner's violence profile, now in its second year of development. Analyzing data collected between 1967 and 1972 (involving 618 programs, 5,790 characters and 3,022 violent episodes), Dr. Gerbner was able to report: "We can see . . . a decline in violent characterizations and in killings, but not in the percent of programs containing violence or in the rates of violent episodes. . . ."[22] Although the frequency of violence in children's cartoons had also declined, it was still "very high . . . the crudest, most brutal kind of indoctrination that one can imagine."[23]

Dr. Gerbner added to the data concerning the "risk ratios" he had first presented to the subcommittee two years earlier. He now reported:

> . . . [T]he decline in violent characterizations that we have observed in the Index comes mostly from a reduction among women, and especially violent women. Killing among men even increased. Equally significant is the fact that while male killers always outnumber males killed, female victims of lethal violence are usually more numerous than women killers.

So while the level of male involvement remained constant and the level of female involvement declined, women involved in violence bore a higher and increasing burden of victimization.[24]

Gerbner's report reveals a handicap in linking social science research with policy review. His elaborate analyses of television programs necessarily lag behind the present schedule and future schedules to which the network leaders now point with pride.

One development underscored by the 1974 hearings was that new sponsors for research on television and social behavior were coming forward—among them General Mills, General Foods, and the Eli Lilly Endowment. Dr. Robert Liebert reported to Pastore's committee that the United Methodist Church, with support from the National Council of Churches, the Markle Foundation and NIMH, was initiating an independent Media Action Research Center.[25] This organization, he hoped, would conduct the monitoring and research support to serve as a continuation of the Surgeon General's inquiry. Leo Singer, the aroused president of the Miracle White Company, reported to the senator that his company's refusal to purchase advertising time on violence-prone shows had brought 35,000 letters of support. For Singer, the lesson was clear.

There have been other signs of increasing self-consciousness among advertising sponsors. The Kellogg Company has drastically shifted its television commercials from the "hard sell" toward "consumer-education" messages. A number of vitamin companies have felt obliged to drop advertisements urging children to think of their products as candy. NBC has carried counter-commercials warning children about eating sweets and even suggesting that they should not spend all their time watching television.[26] To a degree, such steps are the result of pressure by the National Advertising Review Board—which announced a "high priority program" to scrutinize children's advertising—and citizen action groups such as ACT and the Council on Children, Media, and Merchandising. The latter group, led by Robert Choate, has produced public service announcements on snacking, sugar, and cavities which a number of stations have now agreed to carry. Clearly, the matter of what a child learns from his television set has become of concern to a wider constituency than ever before.

The Senate hearings ended with Pastore, although more conciliatory, still convinced that "this is a matter that has to be constantly watched." He spoke in a fatherly way to CBS President Schneider: "Our young people are addicted to television. It sells an idea and the question is, is the idea a good one or a bad one? . . . I hope the industry has reached the point where it can be its own watchdog. . . . This Committee has no intention or inclination to censor. . . . But if in the future we have to call you to account, we will."[27]

14

CONCLUSION

Given the way the system worked in the Surgeon General's quest, we find it difficult to put all the blame for shortcomings on particular villains. Each participant operated according to his own definition of his role. Each behaved logically according to his own terms of reference. Broadcasters and program producers, as Chapter 5 makes clear, work to feed the insatiate consumptive needs of the videotube for attention-getting scripts under conditions driving them to use violence almost as an exclamation point before the commercial breaks. In seeking a quick, definitive answer about the impact of violence on children, Senator Pastore expressed an impatience resulting from too many years of dilatory debate on this topic. The Surgeon General and his colleagues felt a bureaucratic caution in trying to build constituent support for this sensitive inquiry. The social scientists, having long been accustomed to famine in this field of research, were not prepared to take advantage of sudden funding. The Surgeon General's Advisory Committee found itself confronted with constraints that seemed to justify the compromises needed to achieve unanimous support for the Report. And this also made indispensable the great conciliatory skills of the Committee's operating director, Dr. Eli Rubinstein.

Once public, the Report was subject to other exigencies. The press, fearful of government intrusions, regularly treats communication problems as not deserving serious news and editorial attention. Broadcasters have become inured to the nagging warfare of charge and countercharge in which the more important objective is to make points rather than achieve understanding. In such an adversary climate, the congressional hearing becomes a struggle for advantage—an ordeal to be endured or, if possible, ignored.

One can explain why everyone behaved as he did. To review the Surgeon General's quest and its aftermath leads us to speculate on how it might have gone better. We have our own ideal for the process by which research might be linked to policy conclusions and policy in turn to action for an area as sensitive as television programming. In the beginning, there would be a planning conference at which government policymakers, media leaders, and social scientists met together to explore thoroughly the problem at issue, review the existing state of knowledge, and carefully chart the mandate for the proposed inquiry. Then, a committee would be appointed, pooling the wisdom not only of leading social scientists but others from government and the media who have expert advice to offer. While specific research might be commissioned to fill gaps or to test hypotheses, the principal effort would be to formulate as clearly as possible the committee's own best judgment. The goal would be to arrive at a statement, true to scientific disciplines, but understandable and persuasive to the general public. Without drawing an artificial line between scientific findings and policy conclusions, the members would express their combined wisdom about the nature of the problem; what should be done; and, equally important, how it should be done.

Once formulated, such a document could serve as a powerful guide to public policy. But it should be subject to the most searching and critical review, both by congressional committee hearings and also by deliberative groups outside government. Our ideal process would involve an important role for press comment but not of the sporadic headline-seeking variety. Once a policy conclusion had been arrived at—for a problem not susceptible to direct government regulation—we would envisage the creation of nongovernmental councils at national and community levels to provide continuing review and follow-up.

What should be the role of social science in this linkage of knowledge, policy, and action? We presuppose ongoing research capable of undergirding large public policy investigations. But we are dubious of the practice of recruiting social scientists into posses searching for quick solutions. This does a disservice both to social science and to public policy. Ideally, the social science community would maintain institutions capable of anticipating the urgent needs of society. The present system whereby social science entrepreneurs are obliged to contract their services on a random basis hardly provides the best use of their time and talents.

Such would be our ideal. We find ourselves critical of the way the system worked in practice. There was the assumption of broadcasters that television does not seriously affect social behavior, and that outsiders should not meddle in their business. This attitude goes squarely against their arguments to advertisers that television is the most powerful medium in the history of mankind for shaping consumer habits. One might expect them to examine the hidden messages of programming, especially for children, with the same assiduous attention to cause and effect that they devote to the delivery of commercials.

Admittedly, probing television's effects raises First Amendment concerns, especially when government officials have shown a cynical desire to intimidate the media. In the climate of the White House war with the networks, this was not an opportune time for the Surgeon General to be involved in so delicate a mission. But the issue remains. For television programming goes to one of society's most urgent problems—how it educates its youth. From the earliest days of the Republic, education has been the subject of social management. The solution is not to declare a no-man's land in exploring television's effects on the young, but to develop more enlightened ways of exploration.

At the same time, we are not comfortable with the present efforts of social science to determine cause and effect. The laboratory and field experiments we have cited reveal all too many limitations. The child has been measured for aggressive behavior after only brief exposures to selected television fare. While it is significant that there should have been discernible differences in behavior—more especially when one weighs the cumulative results of so many experiments—it is more important to know what happens to the child whose television viewing norm is six hours a day, year in and year out. That is *the* significant phenomenon which makes television distinctly different from books, movies, and every other form of communication. Television has become an enveloping environment through which values and life-styles are transmitted. Somehow social science has got to develop better environmental measures if its findings are to be persuasive.

Over forty years ago, Harold J. Laski voiced misgivings that expertise "too often fails to see round its subject. . . . Too often, also, it lacks humility; and this breeds in its possessors a failure in proportion which make them fail to see the obvious which is before their very noses."[1] Advances in the expertise of social science since that time do not invalidate Laski's criticism. Yet, we refuse to join the critics who claim that social science has nothing to say to the policymaker. Better definitions of role and relationship are needed. We applaud the definitions offered by the Social Science Research Council:

> The contribution of the social sciences is not to replace public debate and legitimate political processes but to supplement them by additional information and rational evaluation. . . .
>
> [T]he social scientist cannot be given full responsibility with respect to the policy judgments into which his findings enter. The policy-makers responsible for making such judgments would do well, however, to make as much use as possible of the knowledge that the behavioral and social sciences provide. Greater danger lies, not in science, but in the pitting of one man's subjective judgments against another's. . . .[2]

The debate over television's effects on children is now twenty years old. Yet the obvious need for concentrated, long-range attention to the issue has been met in only a limited, spasmodic way. Relatively few behavioral scientists have recognized the importance of the issue or tried to gain a better understanding of its implications. Violence on television—even on programs aimed at children—continues apace. The industry has taken little direct action and has not invested significant funds in supporting research into television's effects for good or ill.

In other areas identified as requiring scientific evidence—from cancer control to space exploration—the government has invested large sums in the training of persons who can help shape the hard evidence on which to base intelligent public policy decisions. Investment in training and research programs in mass communications studies has been extremely small.

Television's impact on society demands a significant and long-term investment by government, foundations, and the media. The social sciences must participate in seeking answers to difficult problems and must share in the public policy decisions to be made in this field. There is a need for sustained support for a field of study which the scientists themselves must define, and for the development of mechanisms capable of focusing on long-range and short-range needs.

Certain specific research needs must be addressed. There is much work to be done in determining the "third variables" at work which permit some children to view large amounts of television violence with no apparent harmful effects and incline other children towards aggressive tendencies. What are the factors "predisposing" certain children toward aggression? Professor Albert Bandura of Stanford, who has done pioneering work on television and children, questions the assumption that the predisposition to aggression is simply an inherent "child quality." The size of the "predisposed to aggression" group of children has not been explored. Little is known about the effect of television on the very young—two- and three-year-olds—whose "predispositions" are still being shaped.

Even less is known about the ways violence can be portrayed for positive effect and what, in Wilbur Schramm's words, could be "television's moral equivalent of violence." There is scanty but concrete evidence that entertainment television can be constructive. The Surgeon General's Advisory Committee pointed to "the most striking finding" that young viewers of "Mister Rogers' Neighborhood" from families of low socioeconomic status tended to become more cooperative, helpful, and sharing in their daily relations with others. High socioeconomic children showed different responses in the particular studies.[3] Why the difference and what does it mean for future programming?

What is the potential of television? It not only offers but imposes on children vicarious experience in no way comparable to that of earlier generations. As Dr. Ralph Tyler, formerly of the Social Science Research Council, commented:

> In recent years we have become alert to the importance of studying our environment in terms of its functions and the balance among them. Television is an environment. How are its services being prepared? What range of

opportunities are there for children? Any environment that represents for them so many hours a day deserves a research program with a broad perspective—not only in terms of ill effects but of the total need for vicarious experience in growing up. We must begin to think about television as though we were thinking about food or air or water.[4]

Former FCC Chairman Dean Burch, who has proved to be a thoughtful critic of the industry, has commented:

> Although I am troubled about the effects of televised violence on children, I am just as troubled by the fact that television programming at present does very little in a positive way for children. So I am as concerned about the lack of positive effects as I am about negative effects.[5]

Thinking about television as an environment must engage others besides the behavioral scientists. For too long the humanist, disdaining television, has chosen to ignore it. This bespeaks a blindness about our new universe no less baffling than that of post-Columbian scholars who clung to the theory the world was flat. We must make more meaningful comparisons between the video culture and the print culture. We need to assess television's potential for communicating awareness of man's history, of his great ideas, of human relationships, and of techniques of problem-solving.

Merely listing television's positive potentials raises fear of manipulating this medium as an instrument of social control. Clearly, there are Orwellian dangers implicit in any effort to determine television's social effects. But we cannot avoid "1984" by merely condemning it. Rather our ambition should be to invent an alternative vision of 1984. The first necessity is to expose our communications system to the bright glare of examination and debate.

The search for better understanding of television's effects will have many twists and turns. Covert messages of violence may prove more destructive than blatant ones. Even efforts at positive programming may raise dilemmas, as suggested by one recent criticism that "Sesame Street" may produce "sensory overkill" for some youngsters who are "organically or environmentally not equipped to handle the flood of electronic stimulation."[6] Amid conflicting evidence, it would be easy to become cynically convinced that this powerful medium cannot be governed other than by competitive forces of the marketplace.

Throughout the long inquiry, many felt misgivings about the policy implications of the Surgeon General's quest. Few could wish the federal government to become the director of television programming, nor are many attracted by the notion that behavioral scientists should make a grand design for the nation's communications system. Pluralism is a matter of faith with most social scientists as with others.

But one clear policy implication of the Surgeon General's Report is that Congress now has more than adequate *scientific* justification for periodic review of what the television industry is doing in both children's programming and the larger area of violent content viewed by children. There is no requirement that a law be passed; indeed, it would be impossible to formulate a clear and sensible statute on the basis of present evidence. Moreover, the First Amendment to the Constitution should operate as a strong restraint in this area of lawmaking. But the lawmakers are not going to ignore the fact that television is a licensed industry operating in the public interest. As Pastore recently warned a group of broadcasters:

> To the extent [that] children's television programming is vulnerable to criticism, I assure you, ladies and gentlemen, the [license] renewal process will always have a climate of uncertainty about it. I hasten to add, this is not a threat on my part. It is merely a recognition that a voice more powerful than the FCC—your audience—will demand an accounting for your stewardship.[7]

The time may be fast approaching, however, when Pastore's "Dutch uncle" pronouncements and even the threat of license forfeiture may be of little avail. Technology—by cable, satellite, cassette, and perhaps ultimately by fiber optics—promises a fissioning of our communication channels. Increased competition could open the way for greater diversity and choice in television viewing. But it could also push program producers to extend ever further the outer limits of audience arousal.

The question is whether the television industry can be made more sensitive and self-conscious about its responsibility. Given the evidence available, there is cause for concern, and good reason for demanding changes. At this stage of our experience with television, warns Dr. Percy Tannenbaum, "to do nothing is to do something."[8]

According to surveys cited earlier, many of those who produce, program, and sponsor television programs—including programs specifically designed for young audiences—are utterly unaware of the social implications of those programs. Those who write programs for the television industry are ignorant of the evidence already available about the effects on children. The communication gap between most television experts and child development specialists is great. The burden should be on the industry to close that gap.

We do not agree with the criticisms of the effort to devise a violence profile by which to measure programming. It will not be easy to perfect such a measure but even the systematic pursuit of better indicators will help create a continuing awareness in parent, producer, and advertiser which could have beneficial results.

The problem demands shared responsibility. Since television for American society is an environment, its beneficial use is not an activity to be left exclusively to government, industry, or citizens' action groups. To realize the potential benefits and avoid the clear hazards, children need the help of parents. The television industry needs the advice of social scientists. And social science needs the support of government and the foundations.

Above all, we need to develop new social institutions for establishing the vital linkages between research and public policy, between policy and action. In no area more than communications is the urgency of this need so apparent.

Almost three years have passed since the Surgeon General issued the Report of his Scientific Advisory Committee on Television and Social Behavior. Perhaps the most succinct conclusion for that enterprise was voiced by Meredith Wilson, director of the Center for Advanced Study in the Behavioral Sciences at Stanford, at a conference sponsored by the Aspen Program on Communications and Society. Figuratively placing himself in the Surgeon General's shoes as a witness before Senator Pastore, Dr. Wilson declared:

> The Report is couched in cautious language because these are scientists who must be responsible to their discipline. It may appear to say less to you than it does to me. I believe the Report confirms the folk wisdom that there is a causal relation between violence on TV and the behavior of children in an anti-social way. I see this confirmation as being about as clear as a scientific

group, given the time allowed them, could have given us. Not only does television incite violence in some who are predisposed to violence, but it is clear to me that violence on TV is a factor in determining this "predisposition." Under these circumstances, I am coming to you as a public agent, required to give my advice. In my judgment, violence is clearly dangerous enough to be called to the attention of Congress, the industry and the public. It merits attention and it requires constructive action.[9]

NOTES

1: INTRODUCTION

1. Letter from Senator Pastore to Secretary Finch, March 5, 1969.

2. *Ibid.*

3. *Ibid.*

4. *Ibid.*

5. As quoted in United States Senate Subcommittee on Communications, *Hearings on the Surgeon General's Report by the Scientific Advisory Committee on Television and Social Behavior* (Washington: Government Printing Office, March 21–24, 1972), p. 5.

6. See James D. Halloran and Paul Croll, "Television Programs in Great Britain: Content and Control (A Pilot Study)," *Television and Social Behavior, Reports and Papers, Volume I: Media Content and Control* (Washington: Department of Health, Education and Welfare, 1972), pp. 415–492.

7. James Q. Wilson, "Violence, pornography and social science," *The Public Interest*, Winter 1971, p. 61.

2: ORIGINS OF CONCERN

1. E.B. White, "Removal," *One Man's Meat* (New York: Harper and Brothers, 1938), pp. 3–4.

2. Wilbur Schramm, Jack Lyle and Edwin B. Parker, *Television in the Lives of our Children* (Stanford: Stanford University Press, 1961), p. 11.

3. "Nielsen Geographic Regions Summary," *Television Factbook,* No. 43, Services Volume (1973–1974), p. 102-a.

4. *Television and Growing Up: The Impact of Televised Violence,* Report to the Surgeon General of the United States Public Health Service from the Surgeon General's Scientific Advisory Committee on Television and Social Behavior (Washington: Government Printing Office, 1971), p. 2.

5. Surgeon General's Scientific Advisory Committee on Television and Social Behavior, *Initial Operations, June-October 1969,* submitted by Surgeon General Steinfeld to Pastore Committee (Washington: National Institute of Mental Health, 1969), pp. 2–3.

6. See United States Senate Committee on the Judiciary, "Television and juvenile delinquency," *Investigation of Juvenile Delinquency in the United States,* 84th Congress, 2nd session, January 16, 1956, Report no. 1466.

7. Surgeon General's Scientific Advisory Committee on Television and Social Behavior, *op. cit.,* p. 3.

8. As quoted in Schramm, Lyle and Parker, *op. cit.,* p. 5.

9. *Ibid.,* p. 6.

10. *Ibid.,* p. 1.

11. Surgeon General's Scientific Advisory Committee on Television and Social Behavior, *op. cit.,* p. 4.

12. *Ibid.*

13. As quoted in Schramm, Lyle and Parker, *op. cit.,* p. 4.

14. National Commission on the Causes and Prevention of Violence, "Mass Media Hearings," *Mass Media and Violence,* Volume 9–A (December 1969), Preface.

15. *Ibid.*

16. National Commission on the Causes and Prevention of Violence, *Commission Statement on Violence in Television Entertainment Programs* (September 23, 1969), p. 199.

17. Robert K. Baker and Sandra J. Ball, *Mass Media and Violence*, a staff report to the National Commission on the Causes and Prevention of Violence, Volume 9 (Washington: Government Printing Office, November 1969), p. 381.

18. *Ibid.*, p. vii.

19. *Ibid.*, p. 383.

20. "Curtis Conference on Advertising for Children Brings Heated Exchanges," *Advertising Age*, July 19, 1965, p. 41.

21. Eugene S. Mahaney, "Partners for profit; children, toys and TV," *Broadcasting*, June 30, 1969, p. 18.

22. Robert Lewis Shayon, "Act with ACT," *Saturday Review*, March 7, 1970, p. 22.

23. Editorial, *Christian Science Monitor*, March 24, 1970.

24. Remarks of United States Senator John O. Pastore at the Luncheon Meeting of the National Association of Broadcasters, Shoreham Hotel, Washington, Wednesday, February 28, 1962.

25. *Ibid.*

26. *Ibid.*

27. Letter from Senator Pastore to Secretary Finch, March 5, 1969.

28. *Ibid.*

29. *Ibid.*

3: THE SURGEON GENERAL'S ADVISORY COMMITTEE

1. Interview with Dr. Eli A. Rubinstein, July 1973.

2. See generally Stephen P. Strickland, *Politics, Science, and Dread Disease: A Short History of U.S. Biomedical Research Policy* (Cambridge: Harvard University Press, 1972).

3. See, e.g., Eli A. Rubinstein and George V. Coelho, eds., "Behavioral Sciences and Mental Health: An Anthology of Program Reports" (United States Department of Health, Education and Wel-

fare, Public Health Service, Health Services and Mental Health Association, 1970), Report no. 2064.

4. Another appointee had not been on any of the formal lists of nominations, but had been a college teacher of the daughter of the secretary's special consultant, Richard Moore.

5. Interview with Dr. Percy Tannenbaum, July 1973.

6. Interview with Dr. Joseph Klapper, May 1972.

7. Matilda B. Paisley, "Social Policy Research and the Realities of the System: Violence Done to TV Research" (Unpublished paper, Stanford University: Institute for Communication Research, March 1972), p. 21.

8. Surgeon General's Scientific Advisory Committee on Television and Social Behavior, *Initial Operations, June-October 1969*, submitted by Surgeon General Steinfeld to Pastore Committee (Washington: National Institute of Mental Health, 1969), p. 1.

9. *Ibid.*, p. 2.

10. *Ibid.*, p. 6.

11. *Ibid.*, p. 8.

12. *Ibid.*

13. Interview with Douglas Fuchs, August 1972.

14. Interview with Dr. Jack Lyle, June 1972.

15. Surgeon General's Scientific Advisory Committee on Television and Social Behavior, *op. cit.*, p. 13.

16. Interview with Dr. Jack Lyle, June 1972.

4: WHAT THE RESEARCHERS FOUND: IN THE LAB

1. Robert K. Baker and Sandra J. Ball, *Mass Media and Violence*, a staff report to the National Commission on the Causes and Prevention of Violence, Volume 9 (Washington: Government Printing Office, November 1969), p. 409.

2. *Ibid.*, pp. 409–410.

3. *Ibid.*, p. 375.

4. *Ibid.*, p. 378.

5. *Ibid.*, p. 397.

6. *Ibid.*, pp. 398–399.

7. *Ibid.*, p. 327.

8. *Ibid.*

9. *Ibid.*, p. 330.

10. *Ibid.*, p. 332.

11. *Ibid.*, p. 336.

12. Surgeon General's Scientific Advisory Committee on Television and Social Behavior, *Initial Operations, June-October 1969,* submitted by Surgeon General Steinfeld to Pastore Committee (Washington: National Institute of Mental Health, 1969), p. 14.

13. *Television and Growing Up: The Impact of Televised Violence,* Report to the Surgeon General of the United States Public Health Service from the Surgeon General's Scientific Advisory Committee on Television and Social Behavior (Washington: Government Printing Office, 1971), p. 61.

14. Surgeon General's Scientific Advisory Committee on Television and Social Behavior, *op. cit.,* p. 13.

15. *Television and Growing Up,* p. 10.

16. *Ibid.*

17. Interview with Professor Robert M. Liebert, May 1972.

18. *Ibid.*

19. *Ibid.*

20. *Ibid.*

21. Robert M. Liebert and Robert A. Baron, "Short-Term Effects of Televised Aggression on Children's Aggressive Behavior," *Television and Social Behavior, Reports and Papers, Volume II: Television and Social Learning* (Washington: Government Printing Office, 1971), p. 186.

22. *Ibid.*, p. 191.

23. Paul Ekman et al., "Facial Expressions of Emotion While Watching

Televised Violence as Predictors of Subsequent Aggression," *Television and Social Behavior, Reports and Papers, Volume V: Television's Effects: Further Explorations* (Washington: Government Printing Office, 1971), p. 25.

24. *Ibid.*, p. 27.

25. *Ibid.*, p. 29.

26. *Ibid.*, p. 39.

27. Bradley S. Greenberg, "Televised Violence: Further Explorations (Overview)," *Television and Social Behavior, Volume V*, p. 5.

28. Seymour Feshbach, "Reality and Fantasy in Filmed Violence," *Television and Social Behavior, Volume II*, p. 319.

29. *Ibid.*, p. 320.

30. Robert M. Liebert, Michael D. Sobol, and Emily S. Davidson, "Television and Aggression: A Discussion," *Television and Social Behavior, Volume V*, p. 358.

31. *Ibid.*, pp. 352–359 *passim.*

32. *Ibid.*, p. 360.

33. *Ibid.*

34. United States Senate Subcommittee on Communications, *Hearings on the Surgeon General's Report by the Scientific Advisory Committee on Television and Social Behavior* (Washington: Government Printing Office, March 21–24, 1972), p. 60.

35. Percy Tannenbaum, "Studies in Film and Television-Mediated Arousal and Aggression: A Progress Report," *Television and Social Behavior, Volume V*, pp. 309–350.

36. Greenberg, *op. cit.*, pp. 12–13.

37. *Ibid.*, p. 13.

38. *Ibid.*, p. 12.

39. *Ibid.*, p. 15.

40. David Foulkes, Edward Belvedere and Terry Brubaker, "Televised Violence and Dream Content," *Television and Social Behavior, Volume V*, pp. 59–119.

41. *Ibid.*, p. 101.

42. Greenberg, *op. cit.*, p. 8.

43. James Q. Wilson, "Violence, pornography and social science," *The Public Interest*, Winter 1971, p. 50.

44. Interview with Dr. Percy Tannenbaum, July 1973.

5: *WHAT THE RESEARCHERS FOUND: IN THE FIELD*

1. Monroe M. Lefkowitz, Leonard D. Eron, Leopold O. Walder, and L. Rowell Huesmann, "Television Violence and Child Aggression: A Followup Study," *Television and Social Behavior, Reports and Papers, Volume III: Television and Adolescent Aggressiveness* (Washington: Government Printing Office, 1971), pp. 35–36.

2. *Ibid.*, p. 36.

3. *Ibid.*, p. 38.

4. *Ibid.*

5. Leonard D. Eron and Leopold D. Walder, "Test Burning: II," *American Psychologist*, Volume 16, No. 5 (1961), p. 238.

6. Letter from Dr. Lefkowitz, August 9, 1972.

7. United States Senate Subcommittee on Communications, *Hearings on the Surgeon General's Report by the Scientific Advisory Committee on Television and Social Behavior* (Washington: Government Printing Office, March 21–24, 1972), p. 155.

8. Lefkowitz et al., *op. cit.*, p. 40.

9. *Ibid.*, p. 44.

10. *Ibid.*, p. 48.

11. *Ibid.*, p. 49.

12. *Ibid.*, p. 76.

13. *Ibid.*, p. 84.

14. Aletha Huston Stein and Lynette Kohn Friedrich, "Television Content and Young Children's Behavior," *Television and Social Behavior, Reports and Papers, Volume II: Television and Social Learning* (Washington: Government Printing Office, 1971), pp. 202–317.

15. *Ibid.*, pp. 207–212 *passim.*

16. *Ibid.*, p. 228.

17. *Ibid.*, p. 243.

18. *Ibid.*

19. *Ibid.*, p. 273.

20. *Ibid.*, p. 275.

21. *Ibid.*

22. *Ibid.*, p. 276.

23. Jack M. McLeod, Charles K. Atkins and Steven H. Chaffee, "Adolescents, Parents, and Television Use: Self-report and Other-report Measures from the Wisconsin Sample," *Television and Social Behavior, Volume III*, pp. 239–313.

24. *Ibid.*, p. 240.

25. *Ibid.*, pp. 240–241.

26. *Ibid.*, pp. 244–246.

27. *Ibid.*, pp. 264–270.

28. *Ibid.*, p. 271.

29. *Ibid.*, p. 273.

30. *Ibid.*, pp. 273–274.

31. Jack Lyle, "Children's Use of Television and Other Media," *Television and Social Behavior, Reports and Papers, Volume IV: Television in Day-to-Day Life: Patterns of Use* (Washington: Government Printing Office, 1971), p. 151.

32. Robert B. Bechtel, Clark Achelpohl and Roger Akers, "Correlates Between Observed Behavior and Questionnaire Responses on Television Viewing," *Television and Social Behavior, Volume IV*, pp. 274–299.

33. *Ibid.*, pp. 297–298.

6: WHAT THE RESEARCHERS FOUND: IN THE INDUSTRY AND ON THE AIR

1. George Gerbner, "Violence in Television Drama: Trends and Symbolic Functions," *Television and Social Behavior, Reports and Papers,*

Volume I: Media Content and Control (Washington: Government Printing Office, 1971), p. 35.

2. David G. Clark and William B. Blankenburg, "Trends in Violent Content in Selected Mass Media," *Television and Social Behavior, Volume I*, pp. 197–199.

3. Thomas F. Baldwin and Colby Lewis, "Violence in Television: The Industry Looks at Itself," *Television and Social Behavior, Volume I*, p. 290.

4. *Ibid.*, p. 298.

5. *Ibid.*

6. *Ibid.*

7. *Ibid.*, p. 305.

8. *Ibid.*, p. 323.

9. *Ibid.*, p. 314.

10. *Ibid.*, p. 304.

11. *Ibid.*, pp. 318–319.

12. *Ibid.*, p. 346.

13. *Ibid.*, pp. 321–322.

14. *Ibid.*, p. 348.

15. *Ibid.*, p. 307.

16. *Ibid.*, p. 349.

17. *Ibid.*, p. 306.

18. *Ibid.*, p. 354.

19. *Ibid.*, p. 373.

20. *Ibid.*, p. 359.

21. Muriel G. Cantor, "The Role of the Producer in Choosing Children's Television Content," *Television and Social Behavior, Volume I*, pp. 259–289.

22. Baldwin and Lewis, *op. cit.*, p. 338.

23. *Ibid.*, p. 330.

24. *Ibid.*, p. 351.

25. *Ibid.*

26. As quoted by Myra MacPherson, "Go-Around on Children's TV," *Washington Post,* October 4, 1972.

27. Baldwin and Lewis, *op. cit.,* p. 360.

28. Cantor, *op. cit.,* p. 278.

29. *Ibid.*, p. 279.

30. *Ibid.*

7: REACHING A JUDGMENT

1. "Violence Revisited," *Newsweek,* March 6, 1972.

2. *Television and Growing Up: The Impact of Televised Violence,* Report to the Surgeon General of the United States Public Health Service from the Surgeon General's Scientific Advisory Committee on Television and Social Behavior (Washington: Government Printing Office, 1971), Appendix B, pp. 245–260.

3. *Ibid.*, p. 28.

4. Douglas A. Fuchs, "Television Violence Reinvestigated: The Million Dollar Misunderstanding" (Unpublished memoir), p. 20.

5. *Ibid.*

6. Interview with Dr. Jack Lyle, June 1972.

7. Interview with Dr. Joseph Klapper, May 1972.

8. "Study of TV Violence: Seven Top Researchers Blackballed from Panel," *Science,* Volume 128, No. 3934, May 22, 1970.

9. Letter from Surgeon General Stewart to the president of the National Association of Broadcasters, April 28, 1969. As quoted in *Television and Growing Up,* p. 24.

10. Matilda B. Paisley, "Social Policy Research and the Realities of the System: Violence Done to TV Research" (Unpublished paper, Stanford University: Institute for Communication Research, March 1972), p. 23.

11. *Television and Growing Up,* p. 24.

12. Robert K. Baker and Sandra J. Ball, *Mass Media and Violence,* a staff

report to the National Commission on the Causes and Prevention of Violence (Washington: Government Printing Office, November 1969), p. 281.

13. As quoted in Paisley, *op. cit.*, p. 27.

14. United States Senate Subcommittee on Communications, *Hearings on the Surgeon General's Report by the Scientific Advisory Committee on Television and Social Behavior* (Washington: Government Printing Office, March 21–24, 1972), pp. 156–162.

15. Letter from Dr. Pool to Dr. Lefkowitz, March 1, 1972.

16. *Ibid.*

17. Seymour Feshbach, "Reality and Fantasy in Filmed Violence," *Television and Social Behavior, Reports and Papers, Volume II: Television and Social Learning* (Washington, Government Printing Office, 1971), pp. 337–345.

18. George Gerbner, "Violence in Television Drama: Trends and Symbolic Functions," *Television and Social Behavior Reports and Papers, Volume I: Media Content and Control* (Washington: Government Printing Office, 1971), pp. 62–64.

19. United States Senate Subcommittee on Communications, *Hearings*, March 21–24, 1972, p. 5.

20. *Television and Growing Up*, p. viii.

21. Interview with Dr. Klapper, May 2, 1972.

22. *Ibid.*

23. Robert M. Liebert, "Television and Social Learning: Some Relationships Between Viewing Violence and Behaving Aggressively," *Television and Social Behavior, Volume II*, p. 28.

24. *Ibid.*

25. *Ibid.*, p. 29.

26. *Television and Growing Up*, pp. 18–19.

27. *Ibid.*, p. vi.

8: THE REPORT GOES PUBLIC

1. United States Senate Subcommittee on Communications, *Hearings on the Surgeon General's Report by the Scientific Advisory Committee on*

Television and Social Behavior (Washington: Government Printing Office, March 21–24, 1972), pp. 3–4.

2. United States Senate Subcommittee on Communications, *Scientific Advisory Committee on Television and Social Behavior, Hearings* (Washington: Government Printing Office, September 28, 1971).

3. *Ibid.*, p. 2.

4. *Ibid.*, pp. 2–3.

5. *Ibid.*, p. 5.

6. Jack Gould, "TV Violence Held Unharmful to Youth," *The New York Times*, January 11, 1972, p. 1.

7. *Ibid.*

8. "TV Violence Study Called Whitewash," Washington *Evening Star*, January 18, 1972.

9. "The Violent Strain," *The New York Times*, January 15, 1972.

10. Christopher Lydon, "Hearings to Weigh TV Violence Study," *The New York Times*, January 18, 1972.

11. Tom Shales, "Study Links TV, Child Aggression," *Washington Post*, January 18, 1972.

12. Michael Putney, "TV Gets a Slap, Not a Wallop, for Violence," *The National Observer*, January 29, 1972.

13. As carried in Norman Mark, "Scientists say TV violence DOES influence children," *Birmingham News*, February 7, 1972.

14. "TV Violence Study Called Whitewash."

15. "Violence on air and in life: no clear link," *Broadcasting*, January 17, 1972.

16. United States Senate Subcommittee on Communications, *Hearings*, March 21–24, 1972, p. 267.

17. Robert M. Liebert, "Television and Social Learning: Some Relationships Between Viewing Violence and Behaving Aggressively (Overview)," *Television and Social Behavior, Reports and Papers, Volume II: Television and Social Learning* (Washington: Government Printing Office, 1971), pp. 29–30.

18. Interview with Dr. Robert M. Liebert, May 1, 1972.

19. Linda Charlton, "Study Aides Voice Misgivings About Report on TV Violence," *The New York Times*, February 19, 1972.

20. *Ibid.*

21. United States Senate Subcommittee on Communications, *Hearings*, March 21–24, 1972, p. 134.

22. Charlton, *op. cit.*

23. *Ibid.*

24. United States Senate Subcommittee on Communications, *Hearings*, March 21–24, 1972, p. 19.

25. Dr. Jack Lyle, *An Overview of Research Done for the Scientific Advisory Committee to the Surgeon General of the United States on the Problem of: Television and Social Behavior* (Tokyo: International Congress of Psychologists, August 1972), p. 2.

26. Putney, *op. cit.*

9: NEW HEARINGS, NEW CONSENSUS?

1. United States Senate Subcommittee on Communications, *Hearings on the Surgeon General's Report by the Scientific Advisory Committee on Television and Social Behavior* (Washington: Government Printing Office, March 21–24, 1972), pp. 4–5.

2. *Ibid.*, p. 99.

3. *Ibid.*, p. 26.

4. *Ibid.*

5. *Ibid.*, p. 29.

6. *Ibid.*, p. 47.

7. *Ibid.*

8. *Ibid.*, p. 73.

9. *Ibid.*, p. 72.

10. *Ibid.*, p. 78.

11. *Ibid.*, p. 73.

12. *Ibid.*, p. 65.

13. *Ibid.,* p. 58.

14. *Ibid.,* p. 57.

15. *Ibid.,* p. 59.

16. *Ibid.,* p. 62.

17. *Ibid.,* p. 77.

18. *Ibid.,* p. 142.

19. *Ibid.,* p. 139.

20. *Ibid.*

21. *Ibid.,* p. 181.

22. *Ibid.,* p. 37.

23. *Ibid.,* p. 38.

24. *Ibid.,* p. 35.

25. *Ibid.,* p. 49.

26. *Ibid.,* p. 51.

27. Frederic Hunter, "Violence on TV—What is it doing to our children?" *The Christian Science Monitor,* November 9, 1973.

28. United States Senate Subcommittee on Communications, *op. cit.,* pp. 66–67.

29. *Ibid.,* p. 31.

30. *Ibid.,* p. 105.

31. *Ibid.*

32. *Ibid.,* p. 118.

33. *Ibid.,* p. 116.

34. *Ibid.,* p. 117.

35. *Ibid.,* pp. 118–119.

36. *Ibid.,* p. 121.

37. *Ibid.,* p. 124.

38. Douglass Cater and Stephen Strickland, *A First Hard Look at the*

Surgeon General's Report on Television and Violence (Palo Alto: Aspen Program on Communications and Society, March 1972), p. 11.

39. United States Senate Subcommittee on Communications, *op. cit.*, p. 304.

40. *Ibid.*, p. 305.

41. *Ibid.*, p. 306.

42. Michael Putney, "TV Gets a Slap, Not a Wallop, for Violence," *The National Observer*, January 29, 1972.

10: THE ONSLAUGHT OF THE CRITICS

1. Eli A. Rubinstein, "Televised Violence: The Flaw from the Fortieth View," Communications Colloquium (University of Pennsylvania: Annenberg School of Communications, November 6, 1972).

2. Joseph Morgenstern, "The New Violence," *Newsweek,* February 14, 1972, p. 66.

3. As quoted in Norman Mark, "Scientists say TV violence DOES influence children," *Birmingham News*, February 7, 1972.

4. *Journal of Broadcasting*, Volume XVI, no. 2, Spring 1972, pp. 225–226.

5. *Ibid.*, p. 226.

6. Linda Charlton, "Study Aides Voice Misgivings About Report on TV Violence," *The New York Times*, February 19, 1972.

7. "Violence on air and in life; no clear link," *Broadcasting*, January 17, 1972, pp. 22–23.

8. "Where the buck should stop," *Broadcasting*, April 3, 1972, p. 144.

9. Edith Efron, "A Million Dollar Misunderstanding," Part I, *TV Guide*, November 11, 1972, p. 13.

10. Edith Efron, "A Million Dollar Misunderstanding," Part II, *TV Guide,* November 18, 1972, p. 43.

11. Edith Efron, "A Million Dollar Misunderstanding," Part III, *TV Guide,* November 25, 1972, p. 36.

12. Jack Anderson, "Merry-Go-Round," *Washington Post,* February 10, 1972.

13. "Violence Revisited," *Newsweek,* March 6, 1972, p. 55.

14. Henry Mitchell, "Television Violence," *Washington Post,* March 19, 1972.

15. *Educational Broadcasting Review,* Volume 7, number 2, April 1973, p. 126.

16. *Ibid.,* pp. 124–133 *passim.*

17. George Comstock, *Television Violence: Where the Surgeon General's Study Leads* (Santa Monica: The Rand Corporation, May 1972), p. 3.

18. *Ibid.,* p. 15.

19. *Ibid.,* p. 16.

20. "Feeders at the trough," *Broadcasting,* August 28, 1972, p. 52.

21. Rubinstein, *op. cit.*

22. Leo Bogart, "Warning: The Surgeon General Has Determined That TV Violence Is Moderately Dangerous To Your Child's Mental Health," *Public Opinion Quarterly,* Volume XXXVI, Number 4, Winter 1972–1973, pp. 514–515.

23. *Ibid.,* p. 514.

24. *Ibid.,* p. 516.

25. *Ibid.*

26. Jesse Steinfeld, "TV Violence *Is* Harmful," *Reader's Digest,* May 1973, p. 38.

27. Robert Lewis Shayon, "TV Without Terror," *Saturday Review,* March 4, 1972, p. 34.

11: THE GOVERNMENT'S HESITANT RESPONSE

1. United States Senate Subcommittee on Communications, *Hearings on the Surgeon General's Report by the Scientific Advisory Committee on Television and Social Behavior* (Washington: Government Printing Office, March 21–24, 1972), p. 104.

2. *Ibid.,* p. 184.

3. *Ibid.*, pp. 223–224.

4. Douglass Cater and Stephen Strickland, *A First Hard Look at the Surgeon General's Report on Television and Violence* (Palo Alto: Aspen Program on Communications and Society, March 1972), p. 11.

5. *Ibid.*, p. 304.

6. *Ibid.*, p. 305.

7. *Report of Special Consultation on the Development of Measures of TV Violence* (Washington: National Institute of Mental Health, June 2, 1972), p. 3.

8. *Ibid.*, p. 6.

9. *Ibid.*, p. 4.

10. *Ibid.*, pp. 1–2.

11. Letter from Secretary Richardson to Senator Pastore, July 25, 1972.

12. *Ibid.*

13. Letter from Secretary Richardson to Senator Pastore, August 16, 1972.

14. George Gerbner with the assistance of Michael F. Eleey and Nancy Tedesco, *The Violence Profile: Some indicators of trends in and the symbolic structure of network television drama 1967–1971* (University of Pennsylvania: Annenberg School of Communications, July 1972), p. 1.

15. Bruce M. Owen, *Measuring Violence on Television: The Gerbner Index*, Staff Research Paper, OTP-SP-7 (Washington: Office of Telecommunications Policy, June 1972), p. 4.

16. *Ibid.*, p. 3.

17. *Ibid.*, p. 8.

18. George Gerbner, "Comments on 'Measuring Violence on Television: The Gerbner Index' by Bruce M. Owen" (Unpublished paper), July 13, 1973, p. 1.

19. *Ibid.*, p. 3.

20. *Ibid.*, pp. 3–4.

21. Letter from Secretary Richardson to Senator Pastore, August 16, 1972.

22. *Ibid.*

23. Myra MacPherson, "Talking About TV for Kids," *Washington Post,* October 3, 1972.

24. Liz Roberts, "Trend-analysis of Saturday morning children's programming over twenty years" (Unpublished Federal Communications Commission staff paper), 1973.

25. *TV Guide,* April 21, 1973, pp. 5–6.

26. United States Senate Subcommittee on Communications, *Overview Hearings* (Washington: Government Printing Office, February 22, 1973), p. 41.

27. Interview with Chairman Dean Burch, December 1973.

28. Letter from Senator Pastore to Secretary Weinberger, October 8, 1973.

29. Letter from Secretary Weinberger to Senator Pastore, November 13, 1973.

30. *Ibid.*

12: THE INDUSTRY'S RESPONSE

1. United States Senate Subcommittee on Communications, *Hearings on the Surgeon General's Report by the Scientific Advisory Committee on Television and Social Behavior* (Washington: Government Printing Office, March 21–24, 1972), p. 179.

2. *Ibid.,* p. 181.

3. *Ibid.,* pp. 190–191.

4. *Ibid.,* p. 197.

5. *Ibid.,* p. 217.

6. Interview with Dr. Eli A. Rubinstein, July 1973.

7. Gary Deeb, "TV's September Song," *Saturday Review,* September 9, 1972.

8. *Ibid.*

9. George Gerbner and Larry Gross, *The Violence Profile No. 5: Trends in network television drama and viewer conceptions of social reality* (Univer-

sity of Pennsylvania: Annenberg School of Communications, June 1973), p. 1.

10. *Ibid.*, p. 2.

11. *Ibid.*

12. *Ibid.*

13. *Ibid.*, p. 3.

14. *Ibid.*, p. 2.

15. *Ibid.*

16. *Ibid.*, p. 4.

17. Thomas E. Coffin and Sam Tuchman, "Rating Television Programs for Violence: A Comparison of Five Surveys," *Journal of Broadcasting,* Winter 1972–1973, pp. 15–16.

18. *Ibid.*, p. 16.

19. *Ibid.*, pp. 18–19.

20. Michael F. Eleey, George Gerbner and Nancy Tedesco, "Apples, Oranges and the Kitchen Sink: An Analysis and Guide to the Comparison of 'Violence Ratings'," *Journal of Broadcasting,* Winter 1972–1973, p. 30.

21. *Ibid.*

22. As quoted in "Violence on TV: Why People are Upset," *U.S. News & World Report,* October 29, 1973, p. 33.

23. *Ibid.*

24. As quoted in Edith Efron, "The Children's Crusade that Failed," Part II, *TV Guide,* April 14, 1973, p. 38.

25. "Violence on TV: Why People are Upset," p. 35.

26. *Ibid.*

27. Edith Efron, *op. cit.,* Part I, April 7, 1973, pp. 7–9 *passim.*

28. "Noted Specialists in Educational Planning for Children Named as Consultants in Development and Concepts of Children's Programming on the CBS Television Network," CBS Press release, June 1, 1973.

29. *Ibid.*

30. Interview with Dr. Ithiel de Sola Pool, August 1973.

31. Edith Efron, *op. cit.,* Part III, April 21, 1973, p. 30.

32. Florence Mouckley, "TV Violence Shrinking in U.S.?" *Christian Science Monitor,* November 21, 1973, p. 1.

33. "Dad Declares War on TV Violence," *The Atlantic Monthly,* October 24, 1973, p. 14–B.

34. Frederic Hunter, "Violence on TV," *Christian Science Monitor,* November 9, 1973, p. 13.

35. *Ibid.*

13: POSTCRIPT, 1974

1. Paul Harris, "Pastore Sparks Impact 'Profile'," *Variety,* December 12, 1973, p. 61.

2. United States Senate Subcommittee on Communications, *Hearings on Overview of the Federal Communications Commission,* March 27, 1974, Committee Transcript, p. 169.

3. Cited by Robert Choate, Supplementary Statement to the Senate Communications Subcommittee, March 26, 1974, p. 1.

4. United States Senate Subcommittee on Communications, *Hearings on Violence on Television,* April 3, 1974, Committee Transcript, p. 29.

5. Paul Harris, "TV Violence: Pastore, Present & Future," *Variety,* April 10, 1974, p. 45.

6. *Hearings on Violence on Television,* p. 29.

7. Les Brown, "TV Programming for Fall Cuts Down on Violence," *The New York Times,* April 20, 1974, p. 1.

8. "Children's TV back to a boil among medium's priorities," *Broadcasting,* April 8, 1947, p. 20.

9. *Ibid.*

10. *Ibid.,* p. 21.

11. *Ibid.,* p. 22.

12. *Ibid.*

13. *Variety,* April 10, 1974, p. 45.

14. Louise Sweeney, "Viewers tell Senate probe TV violence still unchecked," *Christian Science Monitor,* April 8, 1974.

15. *Hearings on Violence on Television,* April 5, 1974, p. 272.

16. "Pastore Praises TV For Violence Cutback," *San Jose Mercury,* April 4, 1974.

17. Stanley Milgram, *Television and Antisocial Behavior* (New York: Academic Press, Inc., 1974), p. 68.

18. Melvin Heller and Samuel Polsky, "Summary of the Third Year of Research" on *Studies of Children and Television* (ABC) 1973, p. 5.

19. *Variety,* April 10, 1974, p. 39.

20. *Hearings on Violence on Television,* April 4, 1974, p. 38.

21. *Variety,* April 10, 1974, p. 39.

22. *Statement of George Gerbner prepared for the Hearings of the Senate Subcommittee on Communications Regarding Progress in Developing a "Profile of Violence in Television,"* April 4, 1974 (University of Pennsylvania: Annenberg School of Communications), p. 6.

23. "Violence Hearing Without Thunder of '72," *Television Digest,* April 8, 1974, p. 3.

24. *Statement of George Gerbner,* p. 7.

25. *Hearings on Violence on Television,* April 4, 1974, pp. 157–158; 168–169.

26. "Softening the Hardsell on TV for Children," *San Francisco Chronicle,* May 2, 1974.

27. *TV Digest,* April 8, 1974.

14: CONCLUSION

1. Harold J. Laski, *Fabian Tract No. 235 (1931),* as quoted in "Scholars Examine Value of Social Scientists in Public Policy," *Washington Post,* February 5, 1973.

2. National Academy of Sciences Social Science Research Council, *The Behavioral and Social Sciences* (Englewood Cliffs, N.J.: Prentice-Hall, Inc., 1969), pp. 93 and 128.

3. See generally Aletha Huston Stein and Lynette Kohn Friedrich,

"Television Content and Young Children's Behavior," *Television and Social Behavior, Reports and Papers, Volume II: Television and Social Learning* (Washington: Government Printing Office, 1971).

4. Interview with Ralph Tyler, February 1972.

5. Interview with Chairman Dean Burch, December 7, 1973.

6. "Sesame Street," *San Francisco Chronicle,* November 18, 1973.

7. Remarks of Senator John O. Pastore at the Broadcaster's Meeting at Newport, Rhode Island, October 20, 1973.

8. Interview with Dr. Percy Tannenbaum, February 1972.

9. Douglass Cater and Stephen Strickland, *A First Hard Look at the Surgeon General's Report on Television and Violence* (Palo Alto: Aspen Program on Communications and Society, 1972), p. 11.

INDEX